Transfer of Title Concerning Movables Part III –
Eigentumsübertragung an beweglichen Sachen in Europa Teil III

***Salzburger Studien zum Europäischen Privatrecht***

Herausgegeben von Prof. DDr. J. Michael Rainer

Band 20

PETER LANG

Frankfurt am Main · Berlin · Bern · Bruxelles · New York · Oxford · Wien

Claes Martinson

# Transfer of Title Concerning Movables Part III – Eigentumsübertragung an beweglichen Sachen in Europa Teil III

National Report: Sweden

Edited by Johannes Michael Rainer –
Herausgegeben von Johannes Michael Rainer

PETER LANG
Europäischer Verlag der Wissenschaften

**Bibliographic Information published by Die Deutsche Bibliothek**
Die Deutsche Bibliothek lists this publication in the Deutsche Nationalbibliografie; detailed bibliographic data is available in the internet at <http://dnb.ddb.de>.

The appearance of this book was made possible by the Austrian Science Fund FWF.

ISSN 1435-6090
ISBN 3-631-53949-5
US-ISBN 0-8204-7727-3



www.peterlang.de

Table of Contents

## 1. Introduction

Swedish property law is not regulated by any comprehensive legislation. There is no property law code or civil code dealing with the subject matter. Since the legislators approach in this field has been to regulate only practically important areas the property law is based partly on regulation and partly on case law. The property law has developed through conduct, court practice, by contributions from legal scholars and by conclusions from stray provisions in different legal acts. Where specific practical problems have occurred the legislator has strengthened the solutions by legal acts.

One of the results of this development is that Swedish lawyers generally see concepts as ownership and possession etc. only as functional, generic terms. Though there are different approaches to law in Sweden, as well as in every legal system, the Swedish (Scandinavian) property lawyer generally does not use concepts of this kind substantially – that is as a logical starting point like they represent something existing. In the actual legal problem solving, *i.e.* the concept of ownership has actually not much to do with how property law conflicts are solved. The conflict between two claims for the same property is rather solved by deciding who should be given priority before the other without deciding who should be the owner. Every decision is based on an evaluation of the specific conflict or the type of conflict that the two parties are engaged in. The conflict between the two parties cannot be solved by an investigation of where the ownership is situated. Such an investigation would according to a Swedish approach be seen as unnecessary, metaphysical and as a veil that risks a materially good solution of the real problem.

A programmatic citation from a central Swedish property law monograph can illustrate the general Swedish position:

> "... it should be noted that by claim of ownership nothing else than two things are meant. Firstly, that the claim on B is for specified property, thus not generically defined property. Secondly, that if A wins the conflict, it is ownership that he has to the object, not particular (limited) right. However, *in the talk about A having claims on ownership there is no statement about how the conflict between A and C shall be solved"*.[1]

In addition to this aversion to the application of superior concepts, the traditional ownership terminology has to a large extent been abandoned. If, *e.g.*, there is a conflict between A and B over a certain piece of property, and A wins, the court will, instead of saying that A is the right owner and therefore entitled to the property, say that A has "better right" to the property.[2]

---

[1] See Hessler, H., *Allmän Sakrätt*, Stockholm 1973, s. 64ff.

[2] Rodhe stated, with reference to the different conflicts that may arise in relation between transferor and acquirer and their respective creditors and others that: "the prevailing opinion not

The concept of ownership has been broken down into its elements and it is seen merely as a generic term for all the different rights and obligations that belong to the one we, for the reason of communicative simplicity, call owner.[3] However, instead of talking about the transfer of ownership we talk about the acquirer's protection against the transferor's creditors, the acquirer's protection against other competing acquirers, good faith acquisition and so on.

Thus, Swedish property law could be described as a functional property law. The intention has been (and still is) to avoid solutions based more on deductions from superior concepts and comprehensive codifications than on considerations based on actual circumstances. The aim is to solve property law conflicts by a weighing of the interests considered to be relevant in the particular situation. The functional model is perceived to have a high potential of creating balanced solutions, well adjusted to the specific case at hand. It is also believed to be a model that to a high degree allows the legal practitioners to see not only to the interests of the parties in the dispute at hand, but also to take other relevant interests into consideration.

In connection with this description of the functional model it is important to emphasize that the weighing of interests method does not imply that Swedish property law completely lacks legal rules or that predictability is not considered to be an important factor in the solution of property law problems. Legal rules are of course considered and solutions are often justified (at least partly) by their consistency with other solutions. Analogies play an important rule and the lawyers try to fit their argumentation and decisions into a system. But, compared to the more concept based property law models prevalent in most other European countries, the Swedish functional property law probably to a higher degree emphasizes considerations to real circumstances and aims at creating well adapted, well balanced practical solutions. The practical differences between the approaches are of course hard to evaluate, but theoretically a more direct focus on the interests at hand, should lead to that these interests have more influence.

## 1.1. A few remarks on the historical background

Compared with the property law models prevalent in most other European countries, the Swedish, and to a very large extent Scandinavian, functional model is fairly unique. When examining the origins of the functional property law it becomes clear that the Danish professor Carl Torp presented a functional description of the transfer of ownership as early as 1892.[4] However, it seems as if the breakthrough for the new ideas did not come until after Torp's presentation of

---

only implies that each of the questions at hand are discussed separately, without connection to a certain time of transfer of ownership, but also that one refrains from using the traditional ownership terminology". (Rodhe, K., *Handbok i sakrätt*, Lund 1986, s. 175-176.)

[3] Compare Undén, Ö., *Svensk sakrätt I*, Lund 1973, s. 57.

[4] Se Torp, C., *Dansk tingsret*, Köpenhamn 1892, s. 324.

his ideas at the Nordic lawyers convention 1902. [5] By the critique that was put forward on the convention it is however evident that the traditional, more continental European, substantial view still was prevailing at the time for the convention.[6] There were also (unsuccessful) attempts made to introduce more uniform concepts of ownership by legislation. [7]

That the functional view was successful during the 1910 and 1920's, in spite of critique and warnings as regards insecurity and lack of predictability, is evident from Undén's description of the concept of ownership in his *Svensk sakrätt I*, for many years the standard work on property law.[8] In addition to showing that the functional view had prevailed, Undén's work also expressed the instrumental view on the concept of ownership that more or less is a part of the functional view.[9]

In practice the shift from the substantial to the functional can be supposed to have happened around the same time. This could be illustrated by the cases NJA 1900 s 342, in which the Supreme Court seems to have applied a substantial concept of ownership, and NJA 1925 s 80, in which a functional view seems to have been applied.

In the first case a sales contract regarding a stock of shares had been concluded between a company and a firm. The firm did not pay the price in time, and the company later sold the shares to a third party. The firm then sued the company and invoked its right to buy the shares or to be compensated for the price difference that could arise in connection with the acquisition of the equivalent amount of shares. The District Court rejected the firm's claim since "*the ownership* to the shares cannot be considered to have been immediately transferred to the firm by way of the abovementioned agreement, since the firm never got them into its possession, the firm cannot, on the agreement, base any right to the shares or to their value". The Supreme Court later just confirmed the District Court's ruling.

---

[5] *Forhandlingerne paa det nordiske Juristmöde i Kjöbenhavn 1902*, Köpenhamn 1902 (NJM 1902), s. 137ff.

[6] NJM 1902, s. 153.

[7] See NJA II 1901, s. 1ff. The uniform concepts were suggested to be included in the 1905 Sales Law.

[8] In the years between 1927 and 1973 *Svensk sakrätt I* was the only comprehensive work on property law. Hessler's *Allmän sakrätt* came in 1973, Håstad's *Compendium in Swedish property law* in 1978 and Rodhe's *Handbok i sakrätt* in 1985. In the last few years the supply of Swedish property law works has increased. E.g. Millqvist's Sakrättens grunder, Zetterström's *Sakrättens fyra huvudfall* and Martinson *En struktur över kredit- och exekutionsrätten*.

[9] "The legal concept of ownership contains neither a social program or a natural law idea. Since, from the Government authorities' examination of what the society's and the individuals' interests predict, legal rules on the ownership's extension or limitation have emerged, the law adjusts the concept accordingly. Thus, the ownership is a relative concept and a >>functional concept>>. It is based on applicable legal rules and is used as a formula or a denotation-unit. (Undén 1927, s. 85).

In the latter case the ownership to goods that originally had been given to a bank as a pledge had been transferred to a third party. The bank later sued the buyer and his bankruptcy estate claiming the right to the pledged goods. The District Court ruled in favour of the bank: "even if Bodén [i.e. the pledgor/transferor] was entitled to, as has happened, without the bank's permission sell the goods and the effects, the transfer document has not been treated in the way that is prescribed by K.F. the 20 Nov. 1845 as regards transfer of goods that the buyer leaves with the seller, and the circumstance that Magnusson [i.e. the transferee] has had the keys to the storage rooms ... cannot give him *a better right* than third party ...the District Court decides to ... oblige Magnusson and his bankruptcy estate to ... immediately to the bank give out the effects".

Magnusson and the estate appealed and the Court of Appeal stated: "Since *the ownership* to the goods has been transferred to Magnusson and the goods in question at the time of Magnusson's bankruptcy were in his possession ... [there is] no obligation for Magnusson to give out the goods to the bank ..."

Now the bank appealed, and the judges of the Supreme Court stated: "Even if ... the bank at the time of the mentioned transfer did not have the goods in its possession ... it is obvious that the pledge was for Bodén binding. ... Magnusson's estate has thus no *better right* than Magnusson ... ". The Supreme Court thus ruled in favour of the bank.

Since the end of the 1920's the functional view has been the prevailing view in Sweden. Since then the functional property law has been further developed by jurists such as Hessler, Rodhe and Håstad.[10]

## 1.2. The breeding ground for the functional approach

There are of course a number of different factors that played a role in the "functional breakthrough". One of those factors was the general climate of ideas. At the time there were a strong belief in science, inspired by the enormous success of natural sciences, and old beliefs were called into question. In Sweden we had the Uppsala school of thought, a philosophy that strongly opposed the way in which traditional concepts, such as the concept of ownership, had been used. The Uppsala school's strong influence on Swedish law (giving rise to the Scandinavian legal realism) during a large part of the 20th century probably facilitated the success of the functional property law.

Further, the lack of a comprehensive civil code has probably been a factor of great importance for the Scandinavian approach. This has probably increased the tendency to treat the property law questions more as rather specific problems than as part of a theoretically coherent system.

---

[10] See Hessler 1973, Rodhe 1985 and Håstad 1996.

Another factor that more directly can be presumed to have influenced Torp in his functionalistic thinking was the climate at the law faculty in Copenhagen. At this time the law faculty was both a law faculty and a political sciences faculty. The law professors working at the faculty were thus in close contact with social sciences. Many of them were also involved in legal practice of different kinds. These are circumstances that can be presumed to have facilitated a kind of legal thinking focussed on real circumstances instead of comprehensive legal constructions based on *a priori* defined concepts.
However, the thinkers of the early $1900^{th}$ century only provided the foundation. Most of the solutions from the functional approach have been developed later on. Another aspect of the functional perspective that has been developed later on is the rewriting of the field of norms that is considered to be property law. Modern Swedish lawyers do not hesitate to involve norms from what traditionally is considered as procedural law, penal law or company law into the property law structures.

### 1.3. A peculiar task

From what has been said it is evident that it is a peculiar task to describe how the theme "transfer of ownership" is dealt with in Sweden. The simple answer is that the concept is *not used*. Since we however do have the problems concerning acquirer's protection against the transferor's creditors, the acquirer's protection against other competing acquirers, good faith acquisition and so on, it is possible to tell a story about how we deal with these problems. Considering that the audience for this story is unfamiliar and probably inconvenient with the Swedish structure it might be a good idea to put the questions and structure the story from a more internationally general perspective. The aim of this article is therefore to describe how we solve the factual problems by commenting on some more or less internationally general themes and questions. This will be done with the beginning of chapter 2.
Dealing with questions that are put from a different theoretical background, will to some extent lead to ends that have not been much dealt with in the Swedish legal doctrine. The task therefore involves commenting on quite a few rather "unclear" questions of law. It should therefore be stressed that this story, as stated in the subtitle, is given as *a* Swedish functional approach. Even if we, Swedish and Scandinavian property lawyers, are rather united in a functional scope of approaches, there are of course differences in how we think and how we would prefer to solve a specific problem. Some of us have what you could call a positivistic perspective on law and others have a more realistic conviction. Some of us are interested in the theoretical grounds for how we think and others like to argue more direct.

Thus, it might be; 1) that this article fails in describing all the different ways of thinking, and perhaps especially that Swedish lawyers quite often takes logical short cuts by using the concepts rather substantially, and 2) that some Swedish lawyers will not agree with how a problem is commented in this text even if it seems like a rather simple problem.[11] It should also be pointed out that someone might find a norm or a normative argument that could be argued as relevant for another solution than what is suggested in this article. The priority has not been to make an altogether thorough and detailed examination of the legal sources, but to make a comprehensive story for an international audience.

To somehow illustrate why it is such a peculiar task to comment on questions from a substantial perspective a short introduction to a common structure of Swedish property law will be given.

### 1.4. A Swedish structure of property law problems

A common division in Swedish property law is *the division between the static and the dynamic fields of property law.* To the static field questions could e.g. be counted the questions of the right to use the asset, the right to dispose of the asset, the right to retake the asset, the right to take possession, the right to claim damages and further issues. Static questions are with a Swedish approach seen more as public law than property law questions. The authorities and social codes of conduct limit the ways in which an asset can be used or disposed. To the dynamic field could be counted questions such as whether the parties should be bound against each other, the passing of the risk, whether the responsibility against others should be placed on a certain party, priority over creditors, priority over other acquisitions (third parties) and the right to give someone else the right to use the asset.

The dynamics in the dynamic field is supplied through contracts. Since the Swedish view is not concerned with the transfer of ownership and therefore a contract generally is just an agreement to in some way oblige to another. When the parties bind themselves and enter into the agreement the contract will be decisive for matters that the parties are free to decide about, such as the passing of the risk. To get effects toward third parties concerning responsibility and priority, the parties must fulfil additional measures that vary upon different circumstances. A common such measure is transfer of possession.

The most central effects towards third parties can be reached by agreeing upon specific property. Such agreements constitute property rights (the *rights in rem –*

[11] On the other hand it is probably not a surprise to any legal scholar that lawyers have different opinions on law. Hopefully it is not either a complete surprise that a description of "existing law" is a strange task for some of us, just because the concept "existing law" is a tool that brings some effects that could be valued as predominantly bad.

i.e. rights against things or against a specified part of a person's property). They are usually described with the categories ownership, security rights and usufruct rights, but it should be pointed out that there is no formal *numerus clausus* catalogue in Swedish property law. As already described above, the notion of *ownership* does not include a concept of ownership directly applicable when solving property law problems. However, it is of course used as a concept for ownership acquired through contract of sale and other derivative acquisitions, as well as through occupation and other original acquisitions. The *security rights* would be divided into (1) what could be described as a wide definition of pledge, (2) rights of retention, and (3) a special type of priority to all of a business' movables. *Usufruct rights* might be divided into weak and strong. *Lease* is considered to be a right in rem, albeit a weak or semi-strong one. An old rule is that a sale always breaks a lease. This rule has been abandoned when it comes to immovable property. In doctrine it has also been argued that in some cases a lessee of movables should be protected.
In this context it could also be noted that as regards *the protection of property rights* there are no "types" of actions in this respect. It is possible to ask the court to oblige a counterpart to hand over certain property or to pay damages. The verdict must however be enforceable by the enforcement authority (Kronofogdemyndigheten). It should also be mentioned that *the concept of possession* is used as a signal. The possessor is assumed to be the rightful owner of the property in his possession. A court or authority decision is needed in order to lawfully restore possession to the rightful owner against the possessor's will.
Since property rights can collide and also be in conflict with claims for payment, a structure of two types of conflicts can be created; conflicts between property rights and conflicts between property rights and claims. Each category can be divided in two subcategories.

### 1.4.1. Priority before creditors

A fundamental principle is the *speciality principle*; according to which identification is necessary for rights in rem. Since this principle seems to be common for all western legal systems it should not be a surprising description that this principle is used to sort property rights from obligations. Without identification of the property the claim can only be an obligation.
The speciality principle also entails that it is possible for an acquirer to make the transferor loose his right in rem. Since a movable must be identifiable to uphold a right in rem the transferor will loose his rights if the good is mixed or combined with other property. The transferor will instead get a claim for damages.
With a few exceptions *rights in rem* are not subject to limitation. Obligations, i.e. rights against a part of, or against the whole of, a person's property, are subject to limitation.

#### 1.4.1.1. Priority before creditors for property that the debtor derives from the property rights claimer

The speciality principle is the main requisite used then handling conflicts between a property rights claimer that want to get his property back from the debtor. If the debtor has lent property the owner should get it back even if the debtor cannot pay his debts to other creditors. The property rights claimer (in this case the owner) should be given priority before the general claimants.

Since there is no unitary concept of ownership the question of the effect of a defect regarding an obligation and its effect on the transfer of ownership can be put as - *what happens with the movable if the contract is void or annulled?* A general answer to that question is that the movable should be brought back. If the movable has been merged or mixed with other property the receiver can keep the movable and pay or give compensation. What was once a right in rem has then turned into a claim, (the speciality principle). The invalidity of a contract is in principle given effect against the creditors of the parties. If the seller of a movable has made an invalid contract his creditors can claim the invalidity if the seller is put into bankruptcy.

The seller's possibilities to retake goods when the insolvent acquirer does not pay are dependent on a valid *retention of title*. Retention (or reservation) of title is done through a contractual condition and does not have to be registered. It is generally agreed that such a condition must be made before delivery. It is the right to take the goods back that is retained. The Swedish term for retention of title is "retaking right", but the terminology is not important – the aims of the parties and the function are decisive. It is nowadays considered silly to make a difference between a contractual term that states retention of title / "ownership" and a term that says that the seller should have the possibility to take the good back if the buyer does not pay.

#### 1.4.1.2. Priority before creditors for a property right derived from the debtor

Another important principle in the Swedish property law is the *tradition principle* (traditionsprincipen), used to describe the formalities that an acquirer of chattels generally has to fulfil to get the effects of a right in rem towards others than his counterpart. Depending on the situation and the type of asset, the formalities vary between (1) transfer of possession (tradition), (2) notice to a third party and (3) publicity (marking or registration). In some situations there is no formality requirement at all except that the property must be specialized and identifiable, compare the speciality principle above. During 2002 the Swedish Consumers Sales of Goods Act was changed in this aspect, and nowadays consumers are protected from the moment the contract is closed and the goods are specified, consensus principle. Because of this change to a consensual principle concerning

consumer sales of goods, identification has become a special and new problem. It is in Swedish legal argumentation often supposed that the heaviest argument for a strict use of the tradition principle is to protect creditors from fraud and evidence constructed afterwards.
During a formal *bankruptcy* the debtor looses his right to make decisions concerning his property and his debts. (The Bankruptcy Code is formally applicable to both businesses and private persons but private persons are more seldom put into bankruptcy since it is often impractical and expensive.) The administrator has, as a representative for the creditors and the debtor, the right to terminate contracts. When a contract is terminated the counterpart must claim his rights in the bankruptcy, i.e. get his rights in rem and the bankruptcy dividend for his claims.
There are possibilities to *avoid contracts* (recovery), which are especially damaging for the creditors, in bankruptcy. The formal requirements can be summarized as 1) there must be a formal bankruptcy or business reconstruction proceeding, 2) the contract or the act to be recovered must have been a disadvantage to the creditors, and, 3) the contract or the act to be recovered must have taken place within a certain time before the application for the insolvency proceeding, the time limit vary for different circumstances.
To stress the division between what kinds of rights that are given priority it shall be mentioned that a contractual right of *pre-emption* is not protected in case of bankruptcy of the seller. An illustration of the common belief in the lack of a numerus clausus principle is that, if the future buyer has possession over the movable protection could be argued.

### 1.4.2. Colliding property rights

There are several rules concerning bona fide purchases or *acquisitions in good faith*. For tangibles the principles from old doctrine and practice was manifested through the 1986 Act of Good Faith Acquisition. According to this act it is possible to make a good faith acquisition even if the seller has never been the owner. It is sufficient that the seller has possession and transfers this possession to the acquirer who is in good faith at the time of delivery. For a long time there were no difference made between different sellers. From 1 July 2003 this has however been changed. It is decided that a difference should be made between sellers who got possession to the goods through possession breaking crimes as theft or robbery and sellers who got possession through other ways as lease, lending, deceit, usury etc. The rightful owner may nowadays claim the goods within six months if the purchase in good faith was made from a thief or a robber. There is however a definitive 10-year limit.
As regards *double sales*, a clear general principle is that the first transferee (B) wins as long as the latter (C) has not acquired possession, or equivalent, in good

faith. However, concerning tangibles B has the right to pay C, what he paid or the market price, and in that way get the movable. B:s right to redemption must be used in six months after B was made aware about C:s right and possession.

## 1.5. Disposition

This introductory chapter has been an attempt to in short explain the Swedish functional approach from a Swedish starting point. As have been said the aim of this article is however to describe how we solve the factual problems by commenting on some more or less internationally general themes and questions.

To make an attempt to facilitate to find a comment on a specific topic the article is divided in four parts and 14 chapters. The first Part I on basic information will to some extent already have been explained in this first chapter, but to fulfil the aim to structure the information from a non-Swedish perspective, such comments are given here. Part II on "Derivative acquisitions", Part III on "Original acquisitions" and the very short Part III on "Co-ownership", as well as the 14 chapters are also to some extent overlapping. The reason is to simplify for readers with different interests of the material. A reader interested in for example insolvency could start with chapter 9 on "Consequences of insolvency", and if that chapter is not enough, he could be lead on to chapter 6 on "System of transfer". Other readers could be interested in particular aspects as protection of property rights, double sales, good faith acquisition etc. The themes are all more or less commented from their own starting point. Therefore, with the used structure everyone could hopefully find a short way to what they are looking for and hopefully find enough comments in the section they start with.

There is also another point in all these overlaps. The functional approach is hard for a lawyer with a different approach to understand, even though it actually is a simplification compared to a substantial view. By meeting the approach repeatedly on questions that link with each other, it might be possible to avoid some of the misinterpretations that naturally will occur.

## Part I: Basic information on property law

### 2. Ownership and property rights

#### 2.1. General basics

##### 2.1.1. Characteristics of rights in rem in contrast to obligations

The common way of describing the two types of rights would be:
Rights in rem are rights against things or against a specified part of a person's property. Some rights in rem have priority in bankruptcy, and are with a few exceptions not subject to limitation.
Obligations are rights against a part of, or against the whole of, a person's property. Obligations are subject to limitation. The general period of limitation is ten years, if there is no contact between the parties concerning the obligation. Obligations have the same priority in bankruptcy and therefore get a dividend if there are any assets to divide. Some obligations though have priority in bankruptcy. (This priority has recently, by 1 of January 2004 and in full effect 1 of January 2005, been changed and there are now less priority for banks, landlords and revenue.)[12]

##### 2.1.2. Numerus clausus

There is no formal numerus clausus catalogue. No law or act states or lists such an order. However, an ordinary way of describing the theme would be that there are three major property rights; ownership, security rights and usufruct rights.
To describe the notion of *ownership* in this context one could say that it is used as a concept for ownership acquired through contract of sale and other derivative acquisitions, as well as through occupation and other original acquisitions. Furthermore, the notion of ownership is used in the context of financial leasing and different types of sales with retention of title / ownership.
The *security rights* would be divided into (1) what could be described as a wide definition of pledge, (2) rights of retention, and (3) a special type of priority to all of a business' movables. (This right has recently, by 1 of January 2004, been changed from a floating charge like system to what might better be described as a

---

[12] The new rules are stated in the act of parliament (Svensk författningssamling) SFS 2003:535. Preparatory works consists of the government bill for the new rules Proposition 2002/03:49 and the report (Statens offentliga utredningar) SOU 1999:1. (Acts of parliament can be found in full text under www.riksdagen.se. Government bills and reports can be found in full text under www.regeringen.se. In Swedish with short summaries in English.)

mere dividend and obligation, but since the system still requires possession of a special security paper issued by the Swedish Patent and Registration Office it could also be described as a security right.)

*Usufruct rights* might be divided into weak and strong. Usufruct rights in movables are in general described and treated as weak, i.e. as mere obligations, with the possible exception of a conflict between two lessees where a good faith acquisition could be argued. There is no formal rule to grant a lessee a stronger position but the lessees' interest is nowadays often recognized as important in legal doctrine. In comparison usufruct rights against real estate (land) have in modern time been treated as strong by statute. Against this background it would be possible to say that some usufruct rights in movables will be upheld in bankruptcy, but not against other rights in rem. One example of such a right would be the right of the financial lessee. A division between short term and long-term usufruct rights has not been on the agenda, but could rather easily fit in to the argumentation that has been put forward.

Although there is no numerus clausus catalogue it is sometimes held that there are no other possible rights in rem than the three mentioned, i.e. ownership, security right and usufruct right.[13] In that way a numerus clausus principle could be argued. This is also a pertinent description in so far that the parties of a contract would not be able to decide over the effects of rights in rem. However, a contract must not totally fit into an old concept of rights in rem to be treated as such.[14] New concepts are from time to time recognized in some aspect by the courts. Financial leasing is one such example.[15]

### 2.1.3. General principles of property law

If we by "general principles" mean nothing but useful descriptions of what we like to stress as important interests, or balance of interests, there are some general principles that are often used in property law:

The *speciality principle* (specialitetsprincipen) is used to separate obligations from rights in rem.[16] According to this principle a right in rem should only be upheld when it concerns a thing, which is identifiable and separable. However there are exceptions, especially when a sum of money is held on account for another.

---

[13] E.g. Håstad, Torgny: Sakrätt avseende lös egendom, 1996, p 16, *cited below as Håstad 1996*; Millqvist: Sakrättens grunder, 2000, p 17-18; (/ Rohde: Sakrätt).

[14] Compare Martinson, Claes: Kreditsäkerhet i fakturafordringar, 2002, p 123–153, *cited below as Martinson 2002*, concerning examples on rights in receivables.

[15] See e.g. Möller, Mikael: Civilrätten vid finansiell leasing, 1996, p 118, *cited below as Möller 1996*. Håstad 1996, p 150.

[16] See e.g. Håstad 1996, p 152.

The *tradition principle* (traditionsprincipen) is used to describe the formalities that an acquirer generally has to fulfil to get the effects of a right in rem towards others than his counterpart.[17] Depending on the situation and the type of asset, the formalities vary between (1) transfer of possession (tradition), (2) notice to a third party and (3) publicity (marking or registration). In some situations there is no formality requirement at all. During 2002 the Swedish Consumers Sales of Goods Act was changed in this aspect, and nowadays consumers are protected from the moment the contract is closed and the goods are specified, consensus principle.[18] There is also by statute an exception, i.e. a consensus principle, for negotiable instruments sold by financial institutions.[19]

The term "principle" is also used for themes concerning parts of property law such as security rights in general. Two examples are the invalidity of "lex commissoria" clauses and the right of subrogation. The first is explicitly stated in the Act of Contracts and the other is recognized as a principle in doctrine and practice, (it is also mentioned in the statute concerning the Rome convention of 19 June 1980).[20]

### 2.1.4. Regulation

Concerning movables one could say that Sweden (and the Nordic countries) has a partly regulated, and partly case law based property law. (Land law is more fully regulated.) The statutes concerning movables often deal only with single and rather specific questions and do not have the aim of being part of a complete and coherent system. The oldest existing acts that are still used are from 1734. They regulate some contractual obligations concerning security rights, some questions concerning credit guarantees and a few questions concerning lease.[21] One of the more important regulations, at least theoretically, is the 1845 Bills of sales Act, which contains the formal requirements for the use of registration of some rights in rem (see section 3 below).[22] The Act of Promissory Notes (and claims) and two short acts concerning notice to third parties and beneficial promises are from

[17] The Swedish tradition principle, its history and its european context is dealt with at length by Göransson, Ulf; Traditionsprincipen, 1994.

[18] Konsumentköplagen SFS 1990:932 was changed through SFS 2002:587 and the new § 49; preparatory works – SOU 1995:11, Proposition 2001/02:134.

[19] Promissory Notes Act § 22.

[20] (Act of Contract) – Lag om avtal och andra rättshandlingar på förmögenhetsrättens område, (1915:218), § 37. Rome convention SFS 1998:167.

[21] Handelsbalken SFS 1736:0123.

[22] Lösöreköpslagen; Lag (1845:50 s. 1) om handel med lösören, som köparen låter i säljarens vård kvarbliva.

1936.[23] From the same époque stems an important act concerning priority in accounts.[24]
During the last 30 years there have been various legislating activity – in 1970 and 2003 the rules of priority in bankruptcy and enforcement of claims was reformed,[25] in 1975 came the Act of Penal Interest Rates,[26] in 1978 a new Credit Sales of Goods Act (retention of title),[27] in 1981 the general Act of Limitation[28] and also the grand Enforcement Code,[29] in 1984 the (now abolished) Act of "floating charge",[30] in 1986 the Act of Good Faith Acquisition with important changes 2003,[31] in 1987 the latest Bankruptcy Code,[32] in 1990 a new Special Enforcement Act,[33] and in 1995 a new act for pawn brokers.[34] A more recent legislation is the 1998 Act of Financial Instruments, although it was introduced in a first version in 1989.[35]
Statutes and the official preparatory works can be found in full text, Swedish, on several websites.[36]

## 2.2. Notion of ownership

There is no spelled out, clear and precise, definition of ownership according to Swedish law. Neither is it common to find such a definition in legal doctrine. Nevertheless, "ownership" is a common word in the legal vocabulary and it is used in the legal discourse as well as in everyday language. It is probably best described as denoting a number of legal facts and legal consequences which taken together constitute the notion of ownership. A more down to earth definition would be that ownership is the most unlimited right a person could have over property. The owner has the right or possibility to use his property as he wishes as long as there are no restrictions in law or by agreement. – Characteristically the restrictions in law are however not a common theme in property law concerning

23 Skuldebrevslagen; Lag (1936:81) om skuldebrev, Lag (1936:88) om pantsättning av lös egendom som innehaves av tredje man, Gåvolagen; Lag (1936:83) angående vissa utfästelser om gåva.
24 Redovisningsmedelslagen; Lag (1944:181) om redovisningsmedel.
25 Förmånsrättslag (1970:979) with changes SFS 2003:535.
26 Räntelag (1975:635).
27 Avbetalningsköplagen; Lag (1978:599) om avbetalningsköp mellan näringsidkare m fl.
28 Preskriptionslag (1981:130).
29 Utsökningsbalken.
30 Lag (1984:649) om företagshypotek.
31 Godtrosförvärslagen; Lag (1986:796) om godtrosförvärv av lösöre.
32 Konkurslag (1987:672).
33 Lag (1990:746) om betalningsföreläggande och handräckning.
34 Pantbankslag (1995:1000).
35 Lag om finansiella instrument (1998:1479).
36 The official governmental website is www.regeringen.se. See also www.lagrummet.gov.se, www.riksdagen.se/debatt/sfst/index.asp, www.notisum.se, www.thomsonfakta.se/juridik/.

movables. The question is rather dealt with as a constitutional matter. In the Instrument of Government, which is one of four acts of constitutional character, it is stated that no citizen should be forced to leave his property unless an important public interest requires that, and compensation is paid.[37]

There are several reasons why there is no spelled out definition of ownership according to Swedish law.

First of all, we have to look at the context in which the legal concept of ownership is most relevant; namely transfer of property. As we will see below (under 6.2.) the different problems that may occur in the context of transfer of property are dealt with on their own typical merits. There is no unititular concept of the transfer of ownership. Consequently it has not been meaningful to develop a formal concept of ownership at large. On the contrary, the idea of a formal legal definition of ownership is seen as threatening to obstruct the functional Swedish approach as regards transfer of property.[38]

Secondly, according to the predominant school of legal theory in Sweden during the last century (the Scandinavian realism), although the concept of rights do belong in the legal discourse, it has to be emphasized that rights are not real phenomenon. The justification of a certain legal analysis with reference to a certain right, in the sense that the right has some kind of independent existence, is seen as metaphysical nonsense. Another common opinion has been (and still is) that spelled out definitions of comprehensive concepts, e.g. ownership, are detrimental to legal thinking and development. In a system where legal problems are solved by deduction from superior definitions there is a risk that the solutions do not take the real circumstances into account, thus creating unsatisfactory results. The Swedish approach tends to be functional and to aim at creating legal solutions in which all types of relevant interests has been taken into account.[39]

Finally, a definition of ownership has probably been avoided partly because of its ideological implications. To say, e g, that a person does not have priority over someone else's creditors is maybe perceived as less harsh than if that person's ownership would have been questioned. The conception of ownership has also a general conservative effect, and has therefore been seen as threatening to the reforms that the socialist governments made during the last century.[40]

### 2.2.1. Scope of ownership

There are no interests "linked" to the concept of ownership, but the interests of the "owner" to dispose, to vindicate and to have priority in bankruptcy as well as in

---

[37] Regeringsformen 2:18 (chapter 2 article 18).

[38] Compare Adlercreutz, Axel; Finansieringsformers rättsliga konstruktioner, 2001, p 55–56.

[39] E.g. Håstad 1996, p 209.

[40] E.g. Skogh, Göran / Lane, Jan-Erik: Äganderätten i Sverige, 2000, p 27–28.

other kinds of execution (enforcement), are recognized in a way that could be described as a principle.[41]

When a movable is in the possession of a third party who is bankrupt or the target of execution proceedings, there is a presumption that the movable belongs to the debtor.[42] The owner must prove that he owns the movable. Since the Swedish doctrine of evidence has an informal approach, such evidence could be given in any, convincing, way.

If we should really try to point out something like a "linkage" we could use the example of the right to take property back from someone who has no right to it. The real argument for this solution are seldom discussed or lifted forward. However, this would be to do much of the term "linked interest".

## 2.3. Other property rights in movables

As mentioned above (see 2.1.2.) different concepts of rights in rem are ownership, security and usufruct.

Security rights could out of their characteristics be divided into three; (1) the "pledge" (that is the right to sell the security if the debt is not paid), (2) the rights of retention (that is the right to hold the property as long as the debt is not paid), and (3) the right of special registered priority (företagsinteckning), is the right to get paid a dividend of 55 % in bankruptcy by the outcome of every movable belonging to a business.[43]

The usufruct rights might, as said above, be divided into weak and strong. You could call most forms of financial leasing a usufruct right and it would probably be treated as a strong right that would have priority over other rights. A simple lease for short time would however not. Such a right would probably be treated as a mere obligation.[44]

---

[41] The interest to dispose is recognized through various statutes concerning sales. Vindication is regulated through the Act of Good Faith Acquisition (Godtrosförvärvslagen). Priority in bankruptcy is determined through various principles with the speciality principle as a central concept and the Act Concerning Priority in Accounts (Redovisningsmedelslagen) as an important symbolic statute. The Enforcement Code is based on a recognition of ownership and this is most significant in the rules concerning presumptions for whom should be considered to be the owner if a movable is detected by the enforcement authority (Utsökningsbalken 4:17–23).

[42] Enforcement Code 4:18 (Utsökningsbalken).

[43] A comprehensive book on all sorts of pledge is Walin, Gösta; Panträtt, 1998. The floating charge has as said in 1.1 recently been changed from Företagshypotek to Företagsinteckning. (The former system is described by Walin, Gösta; Företagshypotek, 1995).

[44] Håstad 1996 p 431-437. Möller 1996 p 147-150.

## 2.4. Protection of property rights

### 2.4.1. Actions

As a general principle you could say that there are no "types" of actions in this respect. You can ask the court to oblige your counterpart to hand over a thing or to pay damages. The verdict must however be enforceable by the enforcement authority (Kronofogdemyndigheten). An obligation to do work would therefore in principle not be possible, but this is not a strict principle and pragmatic verdicts are common. There is also a possibility for the court to oblige someone under penalty of fine.

However, there are special summary proceedings for re-vindication. Such an action could be called upon directly at the enforcement authority and could therefore be decided in a fast way (see also below).[45]

It is also possible to get interlocutory injunctions from the court. Thereby anyone could stop another from interfering with his or her rights. An injunction is also decided fast. [46]

The principles concerning actions would belong to the procedural law and civil litigation.[47]

### 2.4.2. Further protection – tort claims and unjustified enrichment

As said above you could ask the court to oblige your counterpart to pay damages for any damage that you have been caused. If your movable has been used by another they must pay for the wear and for the damage you have suffered not being able to use the thing yourself.

You could also argue for damages on the grounds of unjustified enrichment, but there is no general rule in Swedish law on unjustified enrichment, like the one in the BGB. The concept is seldom used in practice. The Supreme Court has probably not used the concept, in a more than peripheral way, since the 1920's.

There is however a couple of stray law provisions, based on the concept of unjustified enrichment. 1) According to the Parental Act a minor does not have the ability to conclude legally binding agreements. If a minor nevertheless concludes an agreement, that agreement is invalid. Normally, the parties to an invalid agreement are obliged to restore each other's performances, or at least recompense the value of the other party's performance. A minor however, is only

---

[45] So called handräckning (help with enforcement) – in accordance to the Special Enforcement Act; Lag (1990:746) om betalningsföreläggande och handräckning.

[46] Rättegångsbalken (Procedural Code) chapter 15.

[47] Rättegångsbalken chapters 13, 15 and 17 kap, and Lag (1990:746) om betalningsföreläggande och handräckning.

obligated to recompense the value of something handed to him by contract to the extent that it has been of use for him.[48] 2) The same rule on compensation applies in the case where an agreement is invalid in accordance with the 1924 Act on Agreements Concluded under the Influence of Mental Illness.[49] 3) There is also a provision, one of the few rules remaining from the 1734 Commercial Code, stating that a principal who is not bound by an agreement concluded by his agent, due to exceeded competence on behalf of the agent, nevertheless is obligated to compensate the other party to the agreement, in the extent to which the agreement has been of use for the principal.[50] 4) Furthermore, the concept of unjustified enrichment is the basis for provisions in the Bill of Exchange Act and the Cheque Act.[51]

The concept of unjustified enrichment has been analyzed in doctrine. According to one view, the general principle of unjustified enrichment is a formula, which hides the lack of rational considerations.[52] (A theme in accordance with the Scandinavian realistic approach.) The concept of unjustified enrichment covers all sorts of solutions based on mere intuition. It is, in reality, nothing but a reference to justice and fairness in general. According to this view, the reason behind the absence of a general principle of unjustified enrichment in Swedish law is the overall absence of constructed definitions of general concepts, and the functional approach aimed at creating practical solutions. It is held to be an advantage that the Swedish Courts have not, in any significant manner, used a general concept of unjustified enrichment. It has contributed to preventing the law from becoming too abstract and divorced from reality.[53] According to another view the concept of unjustified enrichment is however very useful and it is said to be a number of examples on situations in which the concept could be used.[54]

Even if the first view on unjustified enrichment probably is the predominant one, considering the lack of a definition of the concept in law and the insignificant role the concept has played in case law, the concept is sometimes used in legal argumentation and taken seriously by the Courts. In a recent case, concerning the right of recourse between different pledgors, an obiter statement is expressed where the concept of unjustified enrichment is used in order to limit the

[48] Parental Act (Föräldrabalken) Chapter 9, compare chapter 11 (prescribing rules for agreements concluded by incapacitated persons).

[49] Lag (1924:323) om verkan av avtal, som slutits under påverkan av en psykisk störning.

[50] Handelsbalken 18:3.

[51] Växellag (1932:130) 74 §, Checklag (1932:131) 57 §.

[52] Hellner, Jan, in his thesis Om Obehörig Vinst ("On Unjustified Enrichment"), 1950.

[53] Hellner, Jan: Om Obehörig Vinst ("On Unjustified Enrichment"), 1950.

[54] Karlgren, Hjalmar: Obehörig Vinst och Värdeersättning ("Unjustified Enrichment and Compensation"), 1982.

responsibility for the pledgor having disposed of his pledge, without reaping any benefit, in good faith about the other pledgor's right to recourse.[55]

### 2.4.3. Remedies and injunctions

If there are good reasons to believe that someone will interfere the court can oblige that person not to do so under penalty of fine. There are also possibilities for the court to use injunctions.[56]

## 3. Possession

Possession is a word that is used to describe who has got the physical control over the movable. The physical control could however be rather vague, in fact so vague that the concept to some extent also describes where a movable is situated. If the property is in a place where a person normally leaves things without expecting someone to interfere with them, the property is more or less still considered to be in that person's possession.

Possession is not described as a "right". That description it simply not used, even if possession of course is protected. It is naturally not allowed to break the possession of someone else. Possession is protected in the respect that no one, not even the owner can take the thing against the possessors will.[57] Since there in other words do exist legal definitions of what is forbidden, the concept of possession is negatively formed in Swedish law, in the Penal Code. It is forbidden for someone else to interfere with your possession, but the description "right" to be left undisturbed is not made much use of.

To clarify the concept of possession it could also be mentioned that possession in itself does not mean that the possessor have the right to do anything at all with the thing. On the contrary you could argue that mere possession rather obliges you to protect the value of the thing, at least if someone else has an interest in that value.

The word possession is most often avoided when you talk about other property than movables. It is avoided concerning mere rights, such as claims and receivables. Since the Penal Code does use the word possession in the general rules, it has been discussed if mere rights as receivables could be possessed and the interference with such immaterial objects should fall under the rules concerning possession in the Penal Code. The opinions vary.[58]

The concept "animus rem (sibi) habendi" is not used, probably because there has not occurred very many practical problems where the intention to possess has

---

[55] The case NJA 2000 s 129; obiter by Supreme Court judge Torgny Håstad.

[56] Rättegångsbalken (Procedural Code) 15:3.

[57] Brottsbalken (The Penal Code) chapter 8; BrP (Act on promulgation of the Penal Code) 14 §.

[58] See Martinson 2002, p 398–399, and the citations given there.

been viewed as relevant. This theme is however sometimes discussed, see next section.

### 3.1. Forms of possession

The thought of different forms of possession is used and communicated, but only as a simplifying description. So the term intermediary possession (medelbar besittning) is used, but it is just a way to inform about where the property is situated. Compared to other systems this might be an important difference.[59]
A person does not have to keep the movable by himself. He can get the benefits of being possessor with the help of another person.[60] The intention of the other person to possess for the other has not had a significant impact on legal principles or doctrine, but it is sometimes discussed.
If two persons or more have independent access to a movable the description mutual-possession (sambesittning) of property, is used.[61]
If the persons only have access to the movable when they are all together, there is said to be a joint-possession (gemensam besittning).[62]
These two last concepts are not always used in a stringent way and the legislator has used them as if the concept of joint-possession also covers mutual possession.[63] The reason for this vagueness towards these concepts is the functional approach. Since it is not necessary to decide a case as "being" a certain form of possession the concepts are not decisive. If the conflict at hand concerns priority before the creditors of the seller it is more relevant to show that the aims behind the tradition principle are fulfilled, see next section.

---

[59] There might in other systems be distinctions made between different forms of possession based on criteria like (examples from German law):– the intensity of the relationship to the asset: actual physical control (in German law: *"unmittelbarer Besitz"*) – or control only through another person physically holding the asset (*"mittelbarer Besitz"*; the intermediary is called *"Besitzmittler"* in German law, he is *"unmittelbarer Besitzer"* himself).– the intention of the involved persons: possessing the asset "as one's own" (German law: *"Eigenbesitz"*; e.g. the owner, the thief) – or possessing the asset with the intention of someone having some right to use or otherwise hold the asset (*"Fremdbesitz"*; e.g. the lessee, custodian). – social dependence of the person physically holding the asset from the possessor (the intermediary being called *"Besitzdiener"*). – There also might be other criteria like holding the asset in one's own interest or in the interest of another person.
[60] E.g. Håstad 1996 p 50.
[61] E.g. Håstad 1996 p 50.
[62] E.g. Håstad 1996 p 50.
[63] 4:19 Utsökningsbalk (Enforcement Code).

### 3.2. Functions of possession

In Swedish private law possession is used as a signal. The possessor is assumed to be the rightful owner of the property in his possession. The fact that the law protects the existing possession means that it is the party claiming a right to property in someone else's possession that has the burden of proof. A court or authority decision is needed in order to lawfully restore possession to the rightful owner against the possessor's will.
According to the principle of tradition a transferee acquires priority over the transferor's creditors when the possession of the movable has been transferred, see section 6.8. Since this principle is not always easy to use in all circumstances there have been some cases there it has been decided that it should be enough to deprive the transferor his physical control. Thus, it was not necessary for the acquirer to take physical control. The reason argued for this solution is that the main aim should be to deprive the transferor from the possibility to use the appearance of being in full right to give the acquirer property right, see 6.8.
Possession is an important factor when it comes to good faith acquisitions of movables. A buyer can become owner of a movable, bought in good faith, which has been transferred into his possession, only if the seller had the movable in his possession at the time of the acquisition.[64]
A beneficial promise to give away a movable is not binding until the receiver has the gift in his possession. The purpose of this rule is to prevent precipitated promises.[65]
The possessor also has the right to the yield from the property in his possession, provided that he is in good faith regarding his right.[66]

### 3.3. Acquisition of possession

As said above possession is a word that is used to describe who has got the physical control. Acquisition of possession is therefore reached through physical acts. Symbolic delivery and constitutum possessorium are neither accepted nor relevant descriptions.
A description that is used is however intermediary possession, as mentioned above. A third party who is holding the movable could be ordered by the known owner to possess the movable for another instead. This will be accepted as a substitute for the tradition requirement for a buyer to get protection against the seller's creditors. Since the functional approach does not use the concepts as starting points to solve the problems, it will however not necessarily be so that the

---

[64] According to the Act of Good Faith Acquisitions, Lag (1986:796) om godtrosförvärv av lösöre.
[65] Gåvolagen; Lag (1936:83) angående vissa utfästelser om gåva.
[66] Malmström, Civilrätt, 1999, p 85.

known owners order will be given the same effects as possession in all respects. For example it *could* be argued that a good faith acquirer will not always fulfil the possession requirement through such an order.
Another situation where an acquirer can reach effects that he also could have reached through possession is intermediary possession through a document representing the movable. The transfer of such a document is another way to give the holder of the movable an order to possess for the acquirer instead. The transfer of the document could be described as giving the new holder of the document intermediary possession.[67]
From what has been said it could be noted that there are no specific rules governing acquisition of possession. The Penal Code contains rules concerning wrongful acquisition.[68] In property law the most common question concerning acquisition of possession has been whether the former possessor (owner) has lost his possibilities to reach the movable, se above 3.2. If he has not, the movable has been drawn into his bankruptcy. These questions concerning the tradition principle have been decided through court decisions and through reasoning in legal doctrine.[69]

## 3.4. Protection of possession

The Penal Code contains a chapter of rules for protection of possession. These rules protect the holding of and the physical control over the movable.[70] As mentioned above it is argued if mere rights also could fall under this regulation.
As said above, there are special summary proceedings for re-vindication.[71] Such an action could be called upon directly at the enforcement authority and could therefore be decided in a fast way (see also below). There is always an examination of the material legal position if the counterpart demands it. If the claim preliminarily concerns an (interlocutory) injunction the legal position is not examined thoroughly, but on the other hand an injunction would probably never be enforced in a way that transfers possession to the claimant.[72] Possession would most likely be held by the enforcement authority.
The remedies for breaking someone's possession are penal, i.e. fines and imprisonment. As said above the possessor could also be entitled to damages for the wear and for the damage suffered not being able to use the thing.

---

[67] See Sjölagen (Maritime Code) 42-61 §§.
[68] Brottsbalken (Penal Code) chapter 8.
[69] See section 6.8.
[70] Brottsbalken (Penal Code) chapter 8.
[71] According to Lag (1990:746) om betalningsföreläggande och handräckning (Special Enforcement Act).
[72] Rättegångsbalken (Procedural Code) chapter 15.

The entitlement to damages is linked to the fact that damage, afflicted upon the injured person by careless behaviour or by will, has occurred. If a rightful owner unlawfully takes a stolen movable back from a thief and the thief suffers damage in the way described above, there maybe, in some situations, would be a possibility for the thief to receive damages according to the tort law. There is however a strong possibility that these damages would be reduced according to other rules in the tort law, stating that if the injured person has contributed to the damage, the damages can be reduced in accordance with an assessment of what is reasonable.

## 4. Status of rights

The question of status of a right to a movable could be interpreted differently. From a Swedish perspective it could be said that every right to a certain specified object is considered a right in rem and every other right a mere obligation. The division between obligatory rights and rights in rem is of crucial importance considering the effects of the speciality principle and also the more direct remedies that rights in rem are protected with. It is generally also one of the earliest steps in a problem solving analysis to categorise the conflicting rights as one or the other.

Another way to answer the question of status is however that every right is an obligatory right. Some of these obligatory rights will however have certain effects against third parties, and some of these effects are what we say are characteristic for rights in rem. The point in making such a description is to underline that between the parties a right is always obligatory, that is somehow the definition of obligatory right – a right between two parties. This would also be a good description in the respect that if a party refuses and makes it difficult to execute a transfer of the object, the remedy will often be just damages.

Irrespective of the description we use the categorisation of different rights or the decision to give a certain contract a certain effect such as priority before creditors, is an important step in the problem solving analysis. It should therefore be noted that it with a functional approach could be argued that the categorisation should be rather open. In so called hard cases it should not be excluded to come to the conclusion that a certain contract should have some effects that are characteristic for rights in rem and some effects that are characteristic for mere obligations. This is not a common problem at all, but it is of theoretical importance to underline that the functional approach makes the analysis open even on this fundamental point.

It might also be important to mention that the descriptions of property law normally do not take much interest in a systematic division between ways of acquiring rights in rem and obligatory rights. The fact that a contract could give both obligatory rights and rights in rem, and a negligent act typically only an obligatory right, has not been of much interest. Since the functional approach means starting at the problem at hand, it is simply not necessary to structure a description of law from such a starting point.

## 4.1. Lease

Lease is considered to be a right in rem, albeit a weak one or a "quasi right in rem". An old rule is that a sale always breaks a lease. This rule has been abandoned when it comes to immovable property. A person who leases a real estate is protected against the seller's creditors if his right has been registered before the execution right.[73] The lessee is also protected against acquirers of the real estate if the property is sold with reservation for the lessees right, if the lessee has got a written contract and has taken possession of the property or if the acquirer was or should have been aware of the lessees right at the time of the sale.[74] The lease of movables is (with a few exemptions) not regulated by any act or any rules laid down by the Courts.[75] In doctrine it is argued that in some cases a lessee of movables should be protected. Financial leasing is often given as an example.[76]

The short time lease of a car would probably not be given the same position as the financial lease of a car or a machine. Since a short time lease seldom would be a burden the question is not very practical – the short time lease is rather something of value for a buyer and also for the creditors. The circumstances could however sometimes be that the lease is burdening. In these cases the lessee would be entitled to compensational damages for the breach of contract that the original lessor has made by selling the object or by getting bankrupt. It could then be argued that the lessee should have a right of retention – that is the right to hold the object but not use it, until these damages are paid. This question is however not solved and such a right to hold the object would probably not be mentioned or argued at the student textbook level.

If the lessee thinks it is important to protect himself from buyers and creditors, the lessee can demand a security right clause in the leasing contract. With such a clause it would most certainly be possible to both hold and even sell the object to get compensation for damages.

Flats are not in general considered as movables. A rent of a flat is regulated through land law and the typical kind of tenant has a rather strong position – it could be described as a quasi right in rem. The regulation of different leasing rights in land is complex and the protection does in practice depend on several

[73] Utsökningsbalk 12:33, 4:30.
[74] Jordabalk 7:11-14, 7:1. Håstad 1996, p 431.
[75] Håstad 1996, p 431.
[76] Håstad 1996, p 435-437.

circumstances, as for example the creditor's priority to the land. If a flat is rented from a lessee and not directly from the landowner (sub-location), the solutions differ in some aspects. Some would then use the description movable and there are examples from the Supreme Court where they have solved a question more by principles for movables than by land law regulation.
The lease of a hotel room could in principle be analyzed through land law regulation when the hotel building is owned by the hotel business (which is rather seldom the case). Such an analysis would however be rather silly since the practical problems concerning rights to the lease of hotel rooms are solved in a practical manner.

### 4.2. Right of pre-emption etc.

A contractual right of pre-emption is not protected in case of bankruptcy of the seller. However, if the buyer has possession over the movable protection could be argued.[77] Considering the general tradition requirement this is not surprising. Since a buyer is not protected from the seller's creditors when a sales contract has been concluded but the movable still is in the possession of the seller, then the buyer should not be protected when he has got a right of pre-emption. The same arguments apply in both cases. The purpose is to prevent fraud directed against the creditors. When the buyer already has possession the formal condition laid down in order to prevent frauds, i.e. the tradition principle, is fulfilled. There is however no clear answer to this question. The opinions vary.[78]

### 4.3. Indirect representation

There are in principle no differences between direct and indirect representation. The rights of the principal when asset is acquired through an agent are the same as he had acquired himself.

## 5. Field of application and some definitions of property

### 5.1. Field of application

As said there are no unitary rules for transfer of movables. The different aspects that the complex "transfer of movables" consists of are regulated from a functional approach. Different parts of the complex have its own regulation.

---

[77] Håstad 1996, p 442-446.
[78] Håstad 1996, p 442 ff.

These rules differ depending on the kind of movable in question. A list of different movables with their different regulation would be; claims, intellectual property rights, company shares, negotiable instruments, tangibles/chattels, ships, aeroplanes, financial instruments and immovables on land belonging to others. All these are in at least some respect subject to special regulation.[79]

## 5.2. Property definitions

Since the definition of movables is everything that is not immovable or land, movables would cover also animals, money, electricity and gas. However, it would not be possible to draw definitive conclusions out of such a definition. Different kinds of movables will be treated differently.
*Animals* are treated as tangibles in every aspect.[80] It might though be argued that compensational damages should be higher if an animal is a pet with affection value.
*Money* is treated as a special negotiable instrument, but is so special that you could talk about money as constituting its own kind of movable.
*Electricity* and *gas* are in several aspects treated more as services than objects. The content of a tank of gas would be treated as an object, but the delivery of gas through a pipeline would be treated as a service. Electricity would more or less always be treated as a service since there are few containers of electricity of any relevant sizes, (batteries excluded).
The terms tangible / intangible are used only to describe different groups of movables, and not as definitions.
*Tangibles* would be loose things as cars, books, food, petrol etc. *Intangibles* would primarily be intellectual property rights and whatever you would like to call an object which is not manifest by law, such as goodwill. However it is not obvious that phenomenon of this kind should be treated as objects at all.

---

[79] Claims and negotiable instruments mainly through the Act of Promissory Notes. Intellectual property through a few provisions in the different laws on patents and copyright. Company shares through the Act of Promissory Notes. Financial instruments through the 1998 Act of Registration of Financial Instruments. Ships through the Maritime Code (Sjölagen). Aeroplanes through the 1955 Act of Registration of Right to Aeroplanes. (This act is only concerned with pledge of aeroplanes, protection against the seller's creditors when ownership is transferred is unregulated. The buyer is probably protected when tradition has taken place, but the opinions differ.) Immovables on land belonging to others through landlaw (Jordabalken) and case law. In the case NJA 1952 s 407 the Supreme Court decided that the first acquirer is protected from the claims from a later acquirer through the agreement (from this case it has been construed that the buyer also is protected from the seller's creditors by the agreement, see Håstad 1996 p 249). In NJA 1954 s 455 the Supreme Court judged that a pledge is not valid if the building does not come into the buyer's possession.

[80] Though there is a special act for responsibility concerning dogs and cats, Lag (1945:459) om tillsyn över hundar och katter.

"Objectification" of concepts is problematic, especially when it concerns immaterial concepts.[81]

You could of course also call *claims* intangibles, but the point of doing so is not evident. *Negotiable instruments* would be compared to tangibles in most respects, but they are normally treated as a kind of their own. The reason is mostly that claims (receivables) and negotiable instruments are regulated in acts of their own.[82]

[81] E.g. Martinson 2002, p 100–105.

[82] Act of Promissory Notes (Skuldebrevslagen) amongst others.

## Part II: Derivative acquisition

## 6. System of transfer

### 6.1. Basic characteristics

To the extent that you could at all talk about a common Swedish approach it could best be described as an approach where a transfer of ownership concept is not thought of as useful (see above chapter 1. and section 2.2.). On the contrary, it is rather believed that such a concept has negative effects upon legal thinking.
It is however an important part of the picture that the Swedish approach has not always been what it could be described as today. Although there has never been a general rule for transfer of ownership you can historically find old conceptions with both an ownership belief and a more unititular view.[83] The description "transfer of ownership" has been used even during the late 20th century.[84] A general rule for transfer of ownership was also suggested for the 1905 Sales of Goods Act but withdrawn after a remark from the Supreme Court. It was argued that there was no need for such a rule since the different problems were dealt with through considerations of other conditions than ownership.[85] During the 20:th century descriptions as "transfer of ownership" was progressively repudiated as inexpedient.[86] It is hard to say to what extent the different authors and judges were influenced by the Scandinavian theoretical discussion and the "Scandinavian realism", but it is probably correct to say that the realistic approach have influenced even those who do not refer to explicit realistic ideas.[87] Another factor

[83] There has at least not been a rule in the law of 1734 or in statutes thereafter, see Walin, Gösta: Separationsrätt, 1977, p 20. The conception of a substantial ownership concept, acording to which ownership was seen as an entity passing from the seller to the buyer at a certain time, was abandoned in favour of a functional approach that gained ground in the beginning of the last century.

[84] In the standard book on property law of the mid 20:th century Östen Undén in 1927 uses headings as; The transfer of ownership concerning sales of specific goods – Undén, Östen: Svensk sakrätt I, 1927, p 144. He also states that the predominant view is that ownership passes through the contract, p 147. He does however at the same time point out that the question itself (already 1927) was critized as such. Undéns textbook was published in ten editions from 1927 to 1976 and he did even in the later editions not change his headings, but he did strike out the theme about the time of the passing of ownership, see 8:th ed 1973 and 10:th ed 1976 p 94–96.

[85] Undén, Östen: Svensk sakrätt I, 1927, p 146–147.

[86] Hessler, Henrik: Om äganderättsförbehåll och återtagandeförbehåll i 1966 års lag om vad som är fast egendom, in Nordisk Gjenklang Festskrift till Arnholm, 1969, p 459–473. Adlercreutz, Axel: Finansieringsformers rättsliga reglering, 2001, p 55ff. See also the short comment by Hellner, Jan / Ramberg, Jan: Speciell avtalsrätt I Köprätt, 1991, p 354.

[87] It is evident that the realistic approach influenced many Scandinavian authors towards a less conceptual way of thinking, something which is shown in the discussion between the more

that has probably been of great importance for the Scandinavian approach is the lack of a grand codification. Without a systematic codification the questions tend to occur as rather specific and isolated problems. The argumentation then follows that perspective.

The main argument for the repudiation of the transfer of ownership concept is that a unititular concept obstructs the weighing of the relevant interests. All relevant interests cannot be accounted for in a single rule even if several exceptions are made. It is not even a good solution to have a unititular *perspective* on the problems in question. A perspective with one and the same starting point gives an unfounded precedence for some interests and it is coincidence that decides the result. With a unititular concept as starting point the thinking is restrained to formal arguments rather than material. The actual interests are therefore hidden and thereby the unititular concept leads to an unrealistic order. Since law is a living non-static phenomenon, material freedom is also important for every judge who has to deal with a (property law) problem. It is also important for society since the courts otherwise to a larger extent will produce decisions that are divorced from reality.[88]

It is in this context also important to mark that the conception of ownership is heavily burdened by values of a fairly ideological nature. To question someone's ownership can trigger totally different signals and beliefs than a question of however someone should bare the risk or have priority over creditors.

Against the said background it could accordingly be stated that it is a rather strong belief in Sweden (and Scandinavia) that a unititular concept is an inexpedient tool. To use a unititular concept as guidance for so called unclear questions of law is not good at all. To the extent that normative guidance is necessary to handle the problems, such guidance is possible to get from the norms that regulates the different questions of risk, priority etc. In this way the normative support comes from solutions that are closer to the weighing of the interests that are relevant. The result is, at least in theory, a more realistic regulation that is closer to reality.

Compared to a unititular concept the interest of formal predictability is just as good with the Swedish approach. Since the concept of ownership is rather diffuse the unititular concept gives little advantage in this aspect. The predictability in the Swedish approach is also strengthened by the fact that it is clearer for everyone that material considerations have the importance they always, in reality, have.

---

outspoken realists and some of those who did not adopt the realistic approach at full length, see e.g. Lundstedt, Vilhelm: Obligationsbegreppet, Senare delen, Uppsala 1930, p 109–180 criticizing especially Undén, Östen: Några synpunkter på begreppsbildningen inom juridiken, I Festskrift tillägnad Axel Hägerström, 1928.

[88] Compare, concerning the concept freedom of contract and its effects upon the concept of property , Martinson, Claes; Kreditsäkerhet i fakturafordringar, 2002, p 100-104.

### 6.2. The "transfer of ownership"

As said the prevailing Swedish approach could best be described as an approach where a transfer of ownership concept is not thought of as useful. The Swedish approach is instead based upon the view that the different problems within the description derivative acquisition should be dealt with from a more direct weighing of interests.[89] Each problem should be dealt with on its own grounds. Different interests arise in different problems and the solutions should in principle not be affected by the solutions of other problems. The conception of ownership is therefore of rather little interest. It is not relevant to ask who owns.

Who is considered to be "the owner" is a question that to a large extent hides the real interests that has to be balanced wherever a conflict occurs. If you for example have to deal with the conflict between a creditor and a buyer, you should evaluate the typical interests of those two and be rather free in your decision about that norm.[90]

The appropriate questions to be asked (instead of asking when the ownership passes) according to the Swedish approach could mainly be described as under what circumstances; the parties should be bound against each other, the risk should pass, the responsibility against others should placed on a certain party, priority over creditors should be gained, priority over other acquisitions (third parties) should be gained. There are also other questions that could be put under this sphere but they are perhaps seen as even more remote to link to the ownership concept. As follows from the comments these are a bit more strange with a functional approach.

#### 6.2.1. Parties binding against each other

These kinds of questions could be considered contract law questions, but they have severe implications on the questions that come up when working with property law.[91] If e.g. a buyer of a movable goes bankrupt, the seller can in principle separate the movable from the bankruptcy estate if the sales agreement is invalid, see 6.2.9., 6.7., 9.2. and 9.4.3. Since these kinds of questions are relevant for the solutions of the problems that typically occur when dealing with property

---

[89] Håstad, Torgny, Property rights regarding movables, 2000 p 413–414. Håstad 1996, p 209-210.

[90] Håstad 1996, p 209-210. Göransson, Traditionsprincipen, 1985, p 419ff. Compare also Martinson 2002, p 98–100.

[91] This is of course a question that is dealt with in numerous places in doctrine and case law, but the main statute is the Act of Contract (Lag (1915:218) om avtal och andra rättshandlingar på förmögenhetsrättens område).

law, the classification of the question as a contract law or property law question becomes of less interest.[92]

### 6.2.2. Passing of the risk

There are statutory rules for placing of the risk. According to the sales of goods act the risk passes when the goods is left to the buyer or to an independent transport agent. If the seller does not cooperate in the way he should, the risk passes when the seller has done what he should have done to fulfil his delivery obligation.[93]

### 6.2.3. Responsibility against others

Responsibility against others is seen as a tort law issue.[94] As mentioned above the general rule of responsibility in Swedish tort law is based on the culpa principle. If the seller has been negligent he is responsible regardless of "ownership" and regardless of he is seen to have "better right" to the goods than the buyer.
In some cases however the responsibility is strict, regardless of culpa. *One* of these statutes, Act on Supervision of Dogs and Cats, lays the responsibility on "the owner".[95] Others lay the responsibility on "the keeper" (nuclear power), "the producer, importer or seller" (product liability) or on the insurance provider (motor vehicles).[96]
The conclusion is that questions of liability are solved more or less regardless of property law principles. It can also be pointed out that also Swedish tort law have a rather functional approach. Responsibility is laid on the body that is most suitable.

### 6.2.4. Priority over creditors

As mentioned in section 1.4.1.2., the *tradition principle* (traditionsprincipen), is used to describe the formalities that an acquirer of chattels generally has to fulfil to get the effects of a right in rem towards others than his counterpart. Depending on the situation and the type of asset, the formalities vary between (1) transfer of

---

[92] Håstad deals with these kinds of questions in his book on property rights regarding movables. (Håstad 1996, p 203 ff.)
[93] Mainly dealt with in the Sales of Goods Act (Köplagen) § 12–16, but, importantly, also in standard contracts (Incoterms etc).
[94] This question is mainly regulated through tort law. The Swedish tort law is based on a general culpa-principle, see Skadeståndslag (1972:207) 2:1, but there are several different acts concerning torts and liability.
[95] Lag (1943:459) om tillsyn över hundar och katter.
[96] Atomansvarighetslag (1968:45), Produktskadelag (1992:18), Trafiksskadelag (1975:1410).

possession (tradition), (2) notice to a third party and (3) publicity (marking or registration). In some cases such as consumer sales a consensus principle is used instead.
There are also possibilities to *avoid contracts* (recovery) in bankruptcy. Contracts that have been a disadvantage to the creditors can be recovered if they have taken place within a certain time before the application for bankruptcy. The time limits vary between 3 months and 5 years.
The issues on priority over creditors are dealt with without any involvement of an ownership concept. There are of course considerations on the buyer's interest to get what he paid for or the damage he will suffer if he does not get the goods, but these interests are weighed against the creditors interests to get paid and to not suffer from transactions that the seller and buyer just say have taken place. See also sections 6.5.2., 6.8. and 9.2.

### 6.2.5. Priority over other acquisitions (third parties)

As will be dealt with in sections 7. and 11. double sales and bona fide acquisitions are to a rather large extent not dependent of each other. Different interests arise concerning the different questions. The main principle could be described as a priority for the oldest acquisition but with the important exception that the younger acquisition wins if the acquirer made his acquisition in good faith and has fulfilled the relevant requirement; for movables this requirement would be possession or notice to a third party holder of the asset, for claims it would be notice to the debtor, and for shares noted in the computerised register it would be registration.

### 6.2.6. Right to give someone else a right (ownership, security or right to use)

With a functional approach you do not ask at what time a buyer should be able to give someone else a right to the acquired property. The view is in principle that anyone can enter into an agreement where he gives someone a right to a certain property. The question to be asked is more like if there is a point in entering into such a contract. What the acquirer must ask himself is if he will get priority for his right if he acquires from the person he is dealing with. If someone opposes the right of the acquirer, the priority between the acquirer and the opposing party must be tried. In case the acquirer has acquired his right from someone who never had anything to do at all with the movable the acquirer will of course not win, unless he has fulfilled the good faith acquisition requirements.
The crucial question to be asked is in other words either if the acquirer has made a good faith acquisition, or, if the chain of acquisitions is fulfilled at the time when the conflict between the opposing party and the acquirer is tried. It is so to speak possible for the transferor to first give an acquirer a right to a certain property, and

then acquirer the property himself. The order in which the acquisitions are made is not relevant. If the chain of acquisitions is whole when the conflict between the opposing party (the former owner) and the acquirer is tried, the acquirer will be safe.
Since ownership is not used substantially this is not strange. With the functional approach it is not relevant to start with the abstract question who is the owner, and then derive consequences or rights from how that question is decided. Such logic would for the functionalist be a good example on how the real interests are lost and hidden behind legal concepts. When starting with deciding who is the owner, that is a decision typically based on the relation between the transferor, B, and the person he acquired from, A. The interests to be considered in that decision are interests relevant for solving a problem between for example seller and buyer / owner and thief / lessee and sub-lessee. That question will be answered with the influence of interests as who has the better possibilities to minimize the risk for transport damage. Different values embedded in the general social context of ownership will also be given influence.
The real question is however if A has anything to oppose against the right that C claims, (from his agreement with B). In that conflict the interest concerning risk for transport damage has not much to do with the solution. If A is satisfied or not concerned with C:s right, there is no problem. Who is considered to be the owner is not relevant – what's relevant is just who is legally satisfied and who is not.
It could however be noted that a transferor who gives away right to property could commit criminal fraud against the acquirer if he does not get the right he expect. The transferor can also commit embezzlement against someone who risks loosing his right (the rightful owner) because of the transfer. The penal side of the problem has however nothing to do with the property law in this case. If the transferor tells the acquirer that he has not yet bought the property he will not commit a crime.

### 6.2.7. Right to *use* the asset

The right *for the buyer* to use the asset is a question that is seldom addressed in the explicit terms of a right. When the question is dealt with it is typically in the terms of admission, possession and delivery. Since these terms *are* used to specify when the buyer is allowed to begin to use the property it would not be a strange description to instead talk about a right to use. A simple answer is that the parties decide upon the buyer's right to start using. Normally the question is not dealt with expressly, it is implied that the buyer can start use at delivery.
The question of right to use also concerns the question about for how long the seller is allowed to use the property. If the goods have never been used before the answer is of course that the seller has no right to use at all. The goods are then

sold as new and unused. The same argument would apply to second-hand goods that the seller has acquired just to sell in his turn.
However, if the goods are of a kind that the seller uses, the implied term would sometimes be that the seller can use the goods until admission or delivery. If nothing else is said or implied, the seller of a used car can continue to drive the car until delivery.
In some cases the right to use is also explicitly dealt with in the contractual terms. A very common term in consumer sales is a possibility to regret the purchase. The right to use are in these cases limited by the term that the goods must be in the same shape as it was at the purchase. Another common term is retention of title. Such a clause can in some regards limit the right to use. The buyer does not have the right to use the goods in a way that it is consumed or disposed of, not until the goods have been paid.
What have been said concerns how the right to use is divided between two parties. The question of right to use also has another dimension. With a functional perspective, "ownership" is more used in the context of state power and state regulation, – the static field of property law, see section 1.4. The question of right to use could therefore be interpreted as a question of how the citizens are allowed to act. A question of what a citizen should be allowed to do with their property.

### 6.2.8. Right to waste or destroy

The right to dispose of the property in the way of giving another person a right to it, such as security right, right to use or even ownership, is dealt with in section 6.2.6. above. Another disposition is to waste or destroy the property. Disposal of waste is regulated through public law and regards environmental and sometimes moral concerns. To destroy an historical building or a painting just because you own, would for example be something that you might be punished for.
Between the seller and the buyer the right to waste and destroy would much follow the principles mentioned about right to use, section 6.2.7. It is dependant of the circumstances and the aims of the agreement. Sometimes a right to destroy would be against the whole idea of the agreement, i.e. if someone sells a piece of art to a museum. In those cases it could be argued that a right to destroy would not occur before the limitation of the contractual rights for damages for breach of contract. Since the general limitation period is ten years, the right to destroy would occur after ten years.

### 6.2.9. Right to retake the asset (rei vindicatio)

Between the seller and the buyer the right to retake the asset is limited by article 54 § section 4 in the Sales of Goods Act. The seller is not allowed to revoke the contract and take the asset back after the buyer has been given possession. Section

4, 54 § covers by its wordings only the seller's right to take the goods back because of lack of payment. The other article, 55 §, for the seller's revocation of the contract is concerned only with the buyer's lack of cooperation concerning delivery.
Other cases where the seller likes to have the property back are dealt with differently. If the contract is void on a ground according to the Act of Contracts the seller can claim the property back, at least if the buyer caused the void. How far this solution would be used if the buyer gets insolvent is a question of priority before creditors. There has been one interesting case where the buyer could not pay and retention of title was not made, but the Supreme Court gave the seller right to get the goods back because of void, see section 9.2.6.
Another case would be if the buyer breaches the contract after delivery in another way than lack of payment. The buyer could for example promote the goods together with the goods of a competitor to the seller, in a way that the contract does not allow. In such a case the seller will probably be granted the right to take the goods back. (If the contract term is not allowed because of competition law the seller would of course not be given this right.)
The question of right to retake is also relevant in situations concerning property that has been stolen or deprived the rightful owner by other crimes, as when the property is sold by the one who rented it or held the property with the limitation of the seller's retention of title. The right to retake stolen or lost property is limited by the protection the possessor is afforded by the law. The owner has the right to retake stolen property himself in three situations:[97] When a thief is caught in the act, or in close connection to the act; when the property is found to be in the possession of a suspicious person ("lösker man"); and, finally, when the possessor can be suspected of trying to escape. Lost property can be retaken in the two last types of situations. Force may only be used when a thief, caught in the act, tries to prevent the retaking with force or threat of using force.[98]
In other situations the rightful owner has to sue the possessor claiming a better right to the property, although there are summary proceedings to make it easier. The rightful owner has the right to vindicate property if the requirements for a good faith acquisition are not met. If the requirements are met the rightful owner has the right to pay compensation to get his tangible back. See sections 11.1. and 11.8.

### 6.2.10. Right to take possession

The acquirer is entitled to take possession of the movable from the agreed time of delivery or, if there is no agreement, when the payment is made (Zug-um-Zug

[97] 16 § p 6 KF 1864:11 s 101.
[98] Brottsbalk (Penal Code) Chapter 24.

principle). If a movable for some reason is in the possession of someone who is not the owner the owner is not entitled to take possession without consent of the possessor. When the possession is without lawful or contractual support the owner must, as said above, normally sue to get possession.

### 6.2.11. Right to claim damages

As outlined above, the right to claim damages is connected to injury and carelessness. The person who has the right to claim damages does not necessarily have to be the owner.

### 6.2.12. Right to claim compensation for unjustified enrichment

The example, unjustified enrichment, is interesting since it could be said to be an example of a problem partly created by an ownership concept. When the point of departure in the analysis is to decide on ownership, an unjustified enrichment might more often be the case than if the analysis starts with how should the real conflict be decided. It could be argued that unjustified enrichment is a tool that is needed to adjust unreasonable consequences from the ownership point of departure on the problem. With a Swedish functional approach, the concept of unjustified enrichment, is not needed to the same extent, see section 2.4.2.

## 6.3. Differences between types of obligations

The rules concerning the questions of transfer of ownership are not the same for all types of contracts. Nor are they the same for all different kinds of obligations. Although several of the Swedish rules about binding contracts, risk, responsibility and priority are alike, some main differences concern consumer sales and beneficiary obligations.

As said above the Consumer sales of goods act has recently been changed. Consumers are protected against the creditors of the seller from the moment the contract is concluded between the parties and the goods are marked for the consumer.[99] The rule concerning risk is also different between consumer sales and other sales. A consumer normally stands the risk from the moment he gets possession.[100] The rules of risk for other sales are more complex, even though the main rule is that possession is determining also in these cases.[101] (See also section 6.11.)

---

[99] Consumer Sales of Goods Act (Konsumentköplagen) § 49.
[100] Consumer Sales of Goods Act § 8.
[101] Sales of Goods Act (Köplagen) § 12–16.

Contracts are normally binding upon consensus. There are no formalities for a binding sales or security contract. The parties are bound when they have agreed to be bound or one party have reasonable grounds for believing that the other party wants to be bound.[102] To make a beneficiary obligation you must however hand over the movable or a (written) deed of gift. Another way is to make the beneficiary promise in public. As long as the movable is not handed over the obligation can be recalled if the donor gets in economic trouble or the beneficiary treats the donor badly.[103] A beneficiary within marriage does not have to be respected by the creditors of the donor if the donor had fewer belongings than he had debts at the time of the gift.[104] All beneficiary transfers are also especially susceptible to recovery. Beneficiary transactions and other non-business transactions can in the case of bankruptcy be recovered (annulled) within six months. The time limits vary between six months, one year and three years depending on the circumstances.[105]
A claim for damages would not at all concern rules about binding contracts, risk, priority or responsibility for the movable. Such claims are considered to be mere obligations and not rights in rem. They are in other words always claims for money.
As for unjustified enrichment see section 2.4. above.

## 6.4. The basic elements of the "transfer" system

### 6.4.1. "Consensus" and "Tradition"

As mentioned above contracts are normally binding between the parties upon consensus. Transfer of possession (tradition) is a common additional requirement for priority over creditors.

### 6.4.2. "Abstract", "Causal" and "Real agreement"

The descriptions "abstract", "causal" (requiring a valid contract as "cause") and "real agreement" (a declaration or agreement separate from the underlying obligation which is necessary to effect the transfer of ownership), has no function in the Swedish system. In fact descriptions of that kind are hard to even understand from a Swedish perspective.
As described above the Swedish view is not concerned with the transfer of ownership and therefore a contract generally is just a contract. When the parties

---

102 Act of Contract § 1–9.
103 Act of beneficial promises (Gåvolagen) § 1–5.
104 Code of marriage (Äktenskapsbalken) chapter 8.
105 Bankruptcy code (Konkurslagen) 4:6.

bind themselves and enter into the agreement the contract will be decisive for matters that the parties are free to decide about, such as the passing of the risk. To get effects toward third parties concerning responsibility and priority, the parties must fulfil additional measures that vary upon different circumstances. A common such measure is transfer of possession.

If the contract is void it will in principle have no effect on the passing of risk, responsibility and priority. It would with the Swedish approach of course not even be a question if the ownership could pass even though the contract is void or avoided. When the contract is void or avoided the parties are not bound anymore and their performances should be returned or compensation given.

Without a concept of transfer of ownership the "underlying obligation" is of course not of any importance for the view on these matters. When the price is paid in time the seller looses the major ground for revoking. If the price is not paid in time or the performance is void, the contract can be revoked and the performances should be returned. The ownership concept is normally not used in these situations. (In some aspects, such as concerning the compulsory insurance or taxes concerning a car, an ownership terminology might be used to describe who would be obliged to pay, towards the insurance company respectively the revenue, during the period from which the contract was agreed upon until it is revoked. This is however just a way to make it easier to use the terminology of the tax and insurance laws.)

It is also fundamental that the parties should not have the possibility to give themselves a better position against third parties just by using certain provisions or terminology. A clear ambition is to let the function of the contract be decisive for the parties' standing.

### 6.4.3. Synallagmatic contracts

Synallagmatic contracts are treated as other contracts in most respects. There is no requirement of payment to make the contract valid or to get priority over creditors. The term synallagmatic contract is rather topical to underline the interest of the parties to keep their counterpart. A party to a synallagmatic contract could for example be affected negatively if his counterpart sells his future claim before he has fulfilled his part of the contract. If the first party then has to pay the buyer of the claim, the counterpart might have used up his liquidity. According to different doctrines it should therefore be restrictions upon transfers of such claims. The principles are however not very clear.[106]

[106] Martinson 2002, p 206–221, 350–379.

## 6.5. General issues

### 6.5.1. Specific goods – generic goods

The descriptions "specific" and "generic" goods were primarily used in the old Swedish Sales of Goods Act (before CISG), to decide the seller's responsibility for breaches of contract. Nowadays the distinction has little relevance if you by specific goods mean goods that have individual or unique character and by generic goods mean goods that do not have such a character. A relevant distinction which is close to the specific – generic distinction is however the speciality principle, (se above). According to this principle, rights in rem concern only goods that are identifiable. Specific goods are always identifiable. So are also generic goods when separated and individualized, through for example marking.

As follows from what has just been said, identification is necessary for rights in rem. With out identification of the movable the claim can only be an obligation.

For consumer sales of goods identification has become a special and new problem since the change to a consensual principle for protection against the seller's creditors. According to the new law provision a generic good must be separated or marked or specified in a bookkeeping list of the seller.[107] The wording of the new provision does not expressly state who has to do the marking, but it is easy to interpret the text in such a way that it is the seller that ought to do the marking or specification. The effect of a change of the once specified good is not mentioned. A learned guess is that this will constitute, at least a minor, problem when the practical effects of the new rule has to be handled.

The important details of marking and identification have surprisingly not been considered by the legislator.[108] We will probably have to wait and see what the Courts will decide in these matters.

Identification is also necessary for the passing of risk. Before identification of the goods the risk cannot pass to the buyer. As said above the risk often passes upon transfer of possession (tradition).

---

[107] Consumer Sales of Goods Act (Konsumentköplagen) § 49.

[108] It would of course be interesting with an elaborated list of marking and identification in detail. The new Swedish rule was however unfortunately not written against the background of these kinds of experiences from legal system which have dealt with the practical problems. Therefore it is not much to say about the detailed level. The requirements for the "quality" of marking – easy to detect, must it be continuosly marked etc, are not specified or discussed. Neither the requirements for the "quality" of the specification in the bookkeeping so that the asset can be doubtlessly individualised, must it be made in a specific "part" of the bookkeeping system, specific formal requirements regarding the book entry etc.

### 6.5.2. Party autonomy in relation to third party interests

Party autonomy or freedom of contract is a central idea for all property law. It is considered to be a relevant interest to be weighed against other market economy interests such as freedom of competition, freedom of trade, freedom of establishment and consumer freedom.[109] When it comes to the interest of third party protection it is often considered that the contracting parties should not be allowed to affect third parties negatively. The tradition principle has in fact been constructed quite strongly upon a third party protection idea. It is often said that the heaviest argument for a strict use of the tradition principle is to protect creditors from fraud and evidence constructed afterwards.[110] An additional argument is that the tradition requirement protects the creditors from the risk preference that an over indebted debtor has. Since it is rational for such a person to take a huge risk to get a small possibility of avoiding bankruptcy, the possibilities to sell or pawn the goods twice, must be limited.[111]

The tradition principle is used in a quite harsh manner. Sales and security contracts are treated almost the same in this respect. A common argument during the last fifty years has been that the transferor must not be able to get his hands on the movable.[112] The physical possession must be cut off. Exceptions have been very limited, but have been a topical theme in recent years since the Supreme Court has made a few pragmatic solutions, especially concerning claims (receivables). The publicity arising from notice to the debtor has been considered the more important requisite. Small risks for double selling of the claim or of the seller getting his hands on the payment, has not been sufficient to make the notice invalid.[113]

The common belief is a single tradition principle even if this is a description that could be questioned. It would perhaps be better to talk about several tradition principles since it has become evident that the same requirements are not used under different circumstances. The harshness of the physical cut off is differentiated and could be described as balanced against other factors that minimises the risks for third parties. A high level of publicity could for example balance a looser physical cut off.[114]

The concept "forms of tradition" is something else. It is not usual to talk about different forms of tradition. There are however alternative ways under certain

---

[109] See Martinson 2002, p 92–100, and the citations given there.

[110] E.g. Håstad 1996 p 221. Myrdal, Staffan; Borgenärsskyddet, 2002, p 40ff. Folkesson, Enar; Företaget i ekonomisk kris, 2002 p 35–36. See also Martinson 2002, p 275–305, and the citations given there.

[111] See Martinson 2002 p 306-317.

[112] E.g Håstad 1996 p 288ff. Myrdal, Staffan: Borgenärsskyddet, 2002, p 82.

[113] Martinson 2002, p 275–304. Myrdal, Staffan: Borgenärsskyddet, 2002, p 46. See especially the Supreme Court Cases NJA 1986 s 217, NJA 1995 s 367.

[114] Martinson 2002, p 304-306.

circumstances and one could see them as different forms of tradition. One such way is notice to a third party holding a movable instead of a direct taking of possession. Another way is to put a lock on the premises where the movable is placed and give the key to the receiver.
It is in principle also possible to create new forms of transferring possession, forms that have not been thought of before. The decisive requisite is, as said, that the physical possession is cut off.
It can be noted that the consequence of the physical cut off doctrine is that constitutum possessorium cannot be used.[115] Another consequence is that it is not necessary to move, or do anything at all, with a movable that is already in the possession of the receiver when the contract is closed.
It is possible to postpone the binding effects of the contract, in other words to make the contract conditional or optional. To get priority against the creditors, tradition must take place. It is not a problem if tradition is made before the condition is fulfilled. If tradition is made in advance the receiver will get priority from the moment the condition is fulfilled.[116]
(The protection of the seller against the buyer's creditors is another question. Protection for the credit seller is granted only if he has made a valid retention of title and the goods are possible to identify. The requisites for the sellers and other principals' protection are a little complex.)
The main concern has often been to protect creditors from fraud and evidence constructed afterwards. Of main importance are therefore the possibilities to check that a real contract has been agreed. The imprint that tradition, notice or registration brings diminishes the difficulties to check that a certain agreement is not something that the parties have made up afterwards. Publicity is of course another effect of these three kinds of actions, and it is often argued that this publicity gives the creditors information to react upon so that they can terminate their credits and if necessary file for bankruptcy to make recovery proceedings possible.[117] As said an additional and important argument is that the tradition requirement protects the creditors from the risk preference that an over indebted debtor has. The possibilities to double sell and such is minimised through the tradition requirement.
Another argument in favour of the tradition principle and the interests of publicity is that a creditor judges the economic strength of the debtor by viewing what he has in his possession. This argument is considered to be old and of little value

115 The term constitutum possessorium has however been used occasionally to describe a special rule in the Promissory Notes Act that allowes financial institutions to keep negotiable instruments on account for the buyer, see Walin, Gösta: Separationsrätt, 1977, p 18.
116 Håstad 1996 p 221.
117 Folkesson, Enar: Företaget i ekonomisk kris, 2002, p 35-36.

nowadays.[118] Apart from the fact that possession nowadays says little about who has the rights to the objects, a probable explanation is also that the Swedish personal credit report system is rather reliable and informative.[119]
If you compare this with what seems to be the general German and English argumentation, the creditworthiness argument seems to be more highly valued.[120] There are of course a lot of possible explanations to these differences, but institutional differences, as the different personal credit report systems, are probably an important part of the explanation. Another important explanation is probably that lawyers, on each side of the borders, are free to make guesses about socio-economical behaviour. Lawyers are un-contradicted since regulation is the most important institutional factor in these questions. Sociologists and economists therefore have a hard time getting enough standing to get into these debates. An important factor is in other words that predictions of human behaviour made by lawyers, without having conducted sociological or economic studies, have played an important part in the construction of legal rules. If sociological or/and economic studies were to be used to a greater extent, the differences maybe would have been smaller. It is possible that the actual behaviour by, in this case, creditors do not differ very much between the countries.[121]
The tradition requirements have through the years been criticised both as unjust and also as over effective. It has been suggested that the use of the tradition requirement could be compared to "shooting mosquitoes with canons".[122] The recent shift concerning consumer sales is an important reaction upon that kind of critique. It would probably not be very problematic to change the Swedish order and abandon the tradition principle, at least not if the risks for fraud and afterwards constructions are dealt with in the new system. An order of Internet publicity would probably be accepted, but not without a certain degree of anguish.

---

[118] E.g. Håstad 1996 p 211-212. Helander, Bo: Kreditsäkerhet i lös egendom, 1984, p 362f. Myrdal, Staffan: Borgenärskyddet, p 46.

[119] The main regulation is the Act of Personal Credit Information, Kreditupplysningslagen (1973:1173). For an introductory text on the legal and practical aspects on related questions see Edström, Mikael: Inkassohandboken, 1997.

[120] See the argumentation in the English Law Commission's new proposal on Registration of Security Interest.

[121] The arguments for the tradition principle seems to differ to a large extent between different discourses. In German and Austrian literature, and some other, the publicity principle/tradition requirement is traditionally seen as a basis for the creditors to estimate the assets of their debtor. This is highly questionable nowadays. The goals of the tradition requirement most important for Swedish lawyers, to protect creditors from fraud and evidence constructed afterwards, do not seem to be discussed in other legal systems. Neither is the argument that the tradition requirement protects the creditors from the risk preference that an overindebted debtor has. A critical remark concerning all legal argumentation on these topics (and to a large extent also in general), is that lawyers do rather simple assumptions about reality. See also in the main text above.

[122] Håstad 1996 p 212. See also at length Göranson, Ulf: Traditionsprincipen, 1984, p 619ff.

(See also section 6.8. below where the tradition principle is discussed in greater detail.)
Against the background of a criticised tradition principle it is an interesting idea to think of a dispositive tradition requirement. Even though such an idea at the first glance would be considered as rather strange for a Swedish lawyer, it would be something to consider against the real effects that such a principle would have. Since the parties, in different kinds of trade and markets, are well aware of the difficulties with specialisation, the risks of insolvency and the risks for double selling, it might be efficient to let the parties decide. Combined with requirements for specialisation and evidence, such dispositivity could work rather well also in Sweden.

## 6.6. Valid obligation for the "transfer"

### 6.6.1. Contracts

Although a transfer of ownership concept is not used, Swedish lawyers do use terms as ownership, ownership assignment, old owner and new owner etc. It would therefore not be wrong to say that contract is a way to transfer ownership or other rights. The aim could be to simplify the language when describing a possible function of contract. So it would sometimes be quite all right to say that contract is a way to transfer ownership.
There are no limitations as to the types of contracts based in which "ownership" can be transferred. The basis of such a transfer could be sale, barter/exchange, a contract for services e.g. building a ship, financial leasing or a security agreement. Various types of contracts can transfer ownership, in the meaning outlined above.

### 6.6.2. Donations and gifts

Donations and gifts are regulated separately (see 6.3.). The basic concern for this regulation is to protect the donor from being bound by rash promises. As said the donor must hand over the movable or a (written) deed of gift, or make the promise in public. There are also various rules for recovery of gifts to protect the donor's creditors. The passing of risk is of course also a problem that is dealt with differently. The beneficiary must take the gift as it is.[123]

---

[123] An old saying is: 'You should not look in the mouth of the horse when the horse is given to you.' To what extent this value would be prioritized in every situation could be questioned. A more traditional normative argument for this solution would be that the different Sales of Goods Acts explicitly applies to sales and barter, but not gifts. Sales, barters and gifts are otherwise often treated the same and the term 'överlåtelse' is used in legal language to sum up all the three types of transfers.

### 6.6.3. Unilateral promises

The concept unilateral promise has not yet been used in Swedish legal argumentation. A beneficiary promise is regulated by the same principles as for donations and gifts. Promises to enter a contract are binding during the period of acceptance. If other kinds of promises were to be acknowledged as a special kind it would be to underline that there could be reasons to treat them in another way than the ordinary offer – acceptance model.[124] Anyhow, it could be said that unilateral promises is a way to transfer ownership in the same way as contract is.

### 6.6.4. Other obligations[125]

As mentioned above (see 6.3.), claims for damages are mere obligations and unjustified enrichment is a concept that is very seldom used see (2.4.). Damages are in principle only imposed in the form of monetary compensation.

Inheritance, testamentary disposals and division of joint property in marriage are ordinary ways to transfer ownership.[126]

Other kinds of grounds for transfers are bona fide acquisitions, (legal) occupation, specification and res derelictae.[127]

### 6.6.5. Court orders and decisions

When this question occurs it is often said that courts and different public authorities may have some restricted powers to transfer ownership from one subject to the state or to another subject.[128] This may be done only to provide for an important public interest and always against compensation. These kinds of statements probably emanate from the Instrument of Government (Regeringsformen – which is one of four acts of constitutional character), where it is stated that no citizen should be forced to leave his property unless an important public interest requires that, and compensation is paid.[129]

The material regulation that gives the courts the right to transfer ownership consists of expropriation of land (land regulation) and forfeiture in connection to

---

[124] There is an ongoing doctoral thesis project concerning these questions – by Carolina Landys, www.law.gu.se.

[125] Explanation: In some legal systems, such constructions may occur e.g. in double sale cases: A sells first to B – without handing over the asset – and then to C, who acquires possession and therefore, under a tradition system, becomes owner. But under certain circumstances B might have a tort claim against C and this obligation can be the basis for a transfer of ownership from C to B.

[126] See the Code of Inheritance (Ärvdabalk) and the Code of Marriage (Äktenskapsbalk).

[127] E.g. Håstad 1996, p 43-49. Malmström, Åke / Agell, Anders: Civilrätt, 1999, p 85-88.

[128] Malmström, Åke / Agell, Anders: Civilrätt, 1999, p .

[129] Regeringsformen (Instrument of government) 2:18.

criminal acts. The most common decision of this kind is probably made by the Customs at the border.

There is of course also an obligation for courts and authorities to decide who should be considered to be the owner in different situations. Such examples concern bona fide acquisitions, (legal) occupation, specification, res delictae, inheritance, testamentary disposals and division of joint property in marriage. These kinds of transfers are however better described as specific grounds for transfer, se above.

## 6.7. Validity of the obligation

### 6.7.1. Retroactive effect of defects

Without a concept of transfer of ownership the questions concerning validity and such, can be put as – *what happens with the movable if the contract is void or annulled?*

A general answer to that question is that the movable should be brought back. If the movable has been merged or mixed with other property the receiver can keep the movable and pay or give compensation. What was once a right in rem has then turned into a claim, (the speciality principle).[130]

The invalidity of a contract is in principle given effect against the creditors of the parties. If the seller of a movable has made an invalid contract his creditors can claim the invalidity if the seller is put into bankruptcy.[131]

There are a few questions concerning restoration of the effects from void and terminated contracts that are not dealt with very much in theory. One such question is who should get the benefits from the movable during the period that the movable has been in possession of the wrong party. It could be claimed that the old owner should get the proceeds and on the other hand should be responsible for the costs. However this principle must to large extent be dependent on the circumstances, especially who is to blame for the contract being invalid.

It could be claimed that there should be a difference between terminated contracts and void contracts, i.e. contracts that has never been binding (nullities).[132] This is however considered to be more of a theoretical interest. What is relevant are the practical solutions under the different circumstances, and these practical aspects are often more important than the differences that might be between the two concepts. What has to be done is to wind up the parties' relation, to bring the movable to the place where it belongs and to compensate for damages.

---

[130] E.g. Håstad 1996 p 152ff.

[131] Walin, Gösta: Separationsrätt, 1977, p 54–62.

[132] Adlercreutz, Axel: Avtalsrätt I, 1995, p 222-223.

It is however possible to argue that there are differences between terminated and void/avoided contracts as to the protection against the other party's creditors, especially in case of bankruptcy of, or execution proceedings against the buyer, see 6.2.9., 9.2.6. and 9.3.4. When the right for recovery is based on termination, the seller will not get back the movable but only a dividend claim. If the contract were void the possibilities to argue a right in rem would still have some room. The seller would in principle be protected and get his asset back. In the case of non-payment the seller is not protected if he has not declared his interest to revoke when the contract was agreed upon or at least before delivery, (often formed as a retention of title clause).
When it comes to conditional contracts it is even more so that a difference could be stated compared to void contracts. It is rather obvious that the conditional contract has been in effect under a certain time. However, generally speaking, the winding up of these relationships is not in practice very much different from the handling of void and terminated contracts. Variation rather exists because of the very different kinds of circumstances that might be in question, that is different grounds for nullity, different grounds for termination and also different kinds of conditions that a contract might be made dependent upon.

### 6.7.2. Lack of capacity of one of the parties

In addition to what has been said it can here be noted that in case a mentally incompetent party has consumed or otherwise done away with a movable that he did get, he does not always have to give compensation instead (see 2.4.2.). The counterpart has to bare the consequences for having contributed to put the mentally incompetent in a position to handle the movable. The same type of regulation applies when one of the parties to a contract is a juvenile.

### 6.7.3. Mistake regarding solvency

If the party is not solvent or gets insolvent after the contract is closed but before the movable is transferred, the contract can be annulled (terminated). The seller does not have to deliver the movable and also has the right to get the movable back from an independent deliverer, (right of stoppage in transit).[133]
It could theoretically also be claimed that the contract is void if the party is insolvent or otherwise lack economic capacity. The ground could be fraud or immorality.[134]

[133] Sales of Goods Act 61 §. See Johansson, Svante O: Stoppningsrätt, 2001, p 134ff.
[134] Act of contracts § 30 and § 33.

## 6.8. Tradition

As said above (see 1.4.1.2., 2.1.3. and 6.2.4.) the Swedish "delivery requirement", that is the requirement for getting priority against the creditors of the transferor, is manifested through the *tradition principle* (traditionsprincipen). This principle is not laid down in statute. It is a Supreme Court and doctrinal invention, however sometimes claimed to be an "e contrario" interpretation of the 1845 Bills of sales Act.[135]

The main form is of course transfer of possession (tradition), but the other alternative formalities, notice to a third party or publicity (marking or registration), are often also described as requirements stemming from the tradition principle. All these three formalities are considered to create publicity, up to different degrees. Publicity is seen as important (as said, see 6.5.2.) to protect creditors from fraud and evidence constructed afterwards. In some cases the publicity also prevents the debtor from taking the risks of double selling and double pawning, something that actually might seem rational for him to do to try to save himself from bankruptcy.[136] It is also argued that this publicity gives the creditors information to react upon so that they can terminate their credits if necessary.

It is often discussed what is an effective order, (see 6.5.2.). A different regulation that would be seen as an effective instrument to counteract fraud and evidence constructed afterwards would probably be accepted, but to discard the tradition principle would probably create some anguish.

As mentioned above (see 6.5.2.) it is not usual to talk about different forms of tradition. If the main aims behind the principle of tradition (i.e. to counteract fraud, evidence produced afterwards and double selling) are met under the circumstances in question, the measures taken by the parties will be accepted.

To illustrate how the principle of tradition works according to Swedish law, it might be helpful to give a couple of examples. There are numerous cases that illustrate the principle, but here some cases that are referred to in a standard book will be mentioned.[137]

It is not enough that the seller and the buyer in co-operation separate the goods from other parts of the seller's property, if the goods, in some way, stay with the seller. (Except for consumer sales, see 6.3.). The Supreme Court has judged that the buyer should not be protected from the seller's creditors in these kinds of situations. An example of this is the case NJA 1929 s 64. In this case timber was separated and placed on another part of the seller's land, a fact that did not suffice

---

[135] Lösöreköpslagen; Lag (1845:50 s. 1) om handel med lösören, som köparen låter i säljarens vård kvarbliva. The e contrario interpretation is however an argument invented much later than the act, see Göranson, Ulf; Traditionsprincipen, 1984, p 334-336, 352-372.

[136] Martinson 2002 p 306-317.

[137] Håstad 1996 p 221ff.

to protect the buyer. (Timber is now treated in a special law from 1944. The buyer is protected if the timber is marked for the buyer, in accordance with an established custom.)

In the case NJA 1945 s 400 B had contracted with A (a municipal community) to construct a sewer. B was to deliver all the materials for the construction. At the time for delivery and payment B signed a paper transferring the ownership of all the materials to A. The construction materials were delivered to the building site, which was located on property not owned by A, but at A:s disposal. The Court ruled that A was not protected in B's bankruptcy since B did have the actual control over the construction materials and the possibility to freely dispose over it.

Another case, NJA 1975 s 638, in which the Court held that the buyer was not protected, concerned the purchase of a caravan. The buyer had, after the conclusion of the contract, taken the caravan for a test drive. Then the caravan was left on the seller's property for keeping and for some reparations. The buyer was registered in the car register as owner and was handed one of the keys. A few times the buyer let other persons spend the night in the caravan. These measures were not enough to protect the buyer from the seller's creditors. According to the Court the measures could not be considered to manifest, in a sufficiently distinct way, that the seller no longer had the right to dispose the caravan.

In the case NJA 1991 s 564 the seller transferred to the buyer, both a boat and the usufruct right to the property on which the boat was placed (a fact which the land owner was aware of). The Court found that the buyer was protected since the transfer of the property was sufficiently manifested by the transfer of the usufruct right to the property.

The buyer is not protected if the goods are returned to the seller according to a sale and lease back agreement.

In a situation where the transferor and the transferee live together, it can be hard to achieve a manifest transfer of possession (and thus hard to live up to the demands stated by the principle of tradition). The buyer is not protected if the seller possesses the goods in the same way, both before and after the purchase. To protect the buyer from the seller's creditors, persons living together should register the transfer in accordance with the 1845 Bills of sales Act.

To sum up the discussion about tradition; it is the common opinion that, in order for the buyer of a movable to be protected, a transfer of possession (and thus the cutting off of the seller's physical access) must be sufficiently manifest. This in order to protect the creditors by preventing inter alia excessive indebtedness, the possibilities of double selling and the creation of pretence contracts aimed at deceiving the creditors. If the parties do want to leave a tangible in possession of the transferor, it is possible to use registration instead.[138] If the tangible is in the possession of a neutral third party it is sufficient to give notice to that third party.

---

[138] The 1845 Bills of sales Act.

The notice must contain, expressly or impliedly, that the transferor should not be able to get his hands on the good again.

6.8.1. Physical tradition

There is not a single spelled out definition of physical tradition. However (as mentioned in 6.5.2.) a common description would be that the transferor must not be able to get his hands on the movable. The physical possession must be cut off.
In some Supreme Court rulings it has been questioned to what extent the transferor should be able to get his hands on the goods. From the rulings it has been argued that a pawnor might have the possibility to get possession during a limited time for maintenance. It has also been argued that it should not be possible for a person who is on the board of directors of two companies to possess a pledge that one of the companies has given to the other, see the strange case NJA 1972 s 246. The same problem occurs when a sole owner or representative of a company transfers property to the company or vice versa. Since the case 1972 there has been arguments for a physical cutting off principle also in these cases. However, in the case NJA 2000 s 88 the Supreme Court decided that an owner should be given priority in accordance with a floating charge (företagshypotek) that the company board, himself and two others, had granted him. The owner had the letter of floating charge in his home and it could be argued that he therefore had fulfilled the tradition requirements and the cutting off aspect as well – the owner would, as the court pointed out, of course be rather stupid if he let the company pawn the letter to another creditor. According to one of the judges in the case, it should be interpreted as a more general acceptance of a more open tradition requirement in transactions between a company and its owners.[139]
It has also been decided that a buyer of a caravan cannot leave it on the land of the seller even if the buyer gets a key and starts to use it occasionally. On the other hand the Supreme Court has decided that it is sufficient if the buyer of a boat, which is kept on the ground for the winter, tells the landlord that the usufruct right to the berth on land is transferred. The fact that the seller could still get his hands on the boat, as any other person could since the boat was kept on land accessible to the public, should not deprive the buyer from priority over the creditors (see also above).
Since the question of tradition and physical tradition has been very much discussed it is hard to make a clear statement on how the Swedish view should be described. A lot could probably also be said about the characteristics of the

[139] Supreme Court Judge Torgny Håstad, at a seminar in Gothenburg 2002-04-10. Compare Martinson, 2002 p 287-288, 304-306, and Myrdal, Staffan; Borgenärsskyddet, 2002.

Swedish argumentation in these questions.[140] One way of putting it is however that pragmatics has much to do with how the problems are handled. It could also be said that there have been shifts in the argumentation and positions. In the beginning of the last century it would have been said that the consensus principle was the dominating principle. The tradition principle was however on the coming. During the second half of the last century the tradition principle and the doctrine of cutting off grew strong, but only to reach and bite its own tail in the last decade. The cutting off doctrine now seems to be under such influence from pragmatics and consequential argumentation that the tradition principle might better be described as several different tradition principles or requirements, see 6.5.2.

### 6.8.2. "Tradition" by handing over an "instrument"

It would as said (see 6.5.2.) be possible to hand over a key instead of the movable itself. It would also be possible to hand over a document that represents the movable when the movable is held by a third party that is required to give the movable to the holder of the document. What is vital is that the transferor must not be able to get his hands on the movable.

When there is more than one instrument it is hard to state a clear principle. If the circumstances are that a seller or pawnor has locked the movable in on his own premises it would probably be decided that all the keys must be transferred. In that situation the practical possibilities for the transferor to get his hands on the movable would be considered as a too large risk for double selling/pawning. On the other hand it is argued that it is sufficient to transfer one copy of a transport document representing the goods. Here the concerns for a functioning transport system would prevail.[141] Another situation is when there are several third parties that have possession and therefore several parties to give notice. It has been discussed if it is enough to give notice to one of these parties or to all of them. If it is clear to everybody which one of these third parties who should be given notice, it can be argued that it is an effective solution that notice is given only to this party.[142]

If the transferor keeps one key secretly this would in principle not affect the receiver's priority over the transferor's creditors. Although the specific question has not been discussed very often, a balancing of the interests in favour of the receiver would probably be accepted. As long as the receiver has taken reasonable

[140] Some recent statements are made by Lindskog, Stefan: Om denuntiationmsmottagares ansvar, i festskrift till Nordenson, 1999, p 296–297. Myrdal, Staffan: Borgenärsskyddet, 2002, p 234–235. Martinson 2002, p 304–306.

[141] Håstad 1996, p 179. Johansson, Svante O: Stoppningsrätt, 2001.

[142] Martinson 2002, p 313–317.

precautionary measurements to avoid such acts, the receiver should get his priority. Support for this conclusion could be drawn from arguments that says that priority should not be lost if the pawnor gets the object back incidentally.

### 6.8.3. "Tradition" by affixing a sign

In accordance with what has been said about cutting off the possibilities to get the movable back, affixing a sign could only be efficient if a sign would have a cutting off effect. There are probably very few situations, if any, where this is the case. Since the harsh approach to cutting off sometimes creates practical problems it has been discussed if affixing a sign in combination with other measurements could sometimes be sufficient. One example would be when a whole business is sold. If the buyer then takes physical possession of some of the tangibles (and intangibles) and changes the business sign the old owner could still have physical access to the premises, for example if he starts to work as an employee.

Affixing a sign has also been formally acknowledged as a subsidiary form in some situations. There is a special act concerning wood and timber that only requires marking.[143] This could be done with a plasticized paper stapled to the stack.

It should also be noted that if there is a traditional way of handling business concerning a certain movable, where affixing of a sign is the way to deal with the practical problem, this traditional method would probably be accepted by the courts (and most certainly by the typical bankruptcy administrator). Since the use of signs is very limited and justified by pragmatic considerations it is not seen as problematical that the transferor can change the sign. If however there would be a change and the use of signs would be a more general solution, this would probably be seen as very problematical. It is not in line with the strong Swedish concerns regarding fraud and evidence constructed afterwards.

### 6.8.4. Tradition through documents of title

As mentioned above (regarding the transfer of instruments) documents of title are treated as substitutes for the goods as long as the possessor of the goods is required to give the goods only to the possessor of the document. There are a variety of terms that are used in these kinds of documents and the documents are also given several different names.[144]

The belief systems built around these documents are rather interesting since they tend to be given almost magical status. They are however nothing but different sets of contractual terms that could be varied in a number of different ways. These

[143] Lag (1944:302) om köpres rätt till märkt virke.
[144] Bill of lading, Waybill, Confinement note etc.

kinds of contractual constructions are also interesting in regards to the concept of ownership. It is sometimes quite evident that the parties have divided their authorities concerning the goods in such a way that for example the right to direct the goods is a more significant factor to take into consideration than any other "ownership aspect".[145]
One typical kind of condition is that any holder of the document should have the right to get the goods if he presents the document. Another kind is that the holder of the document must be able to show how he did acquire the document. Since these kinds of documents are used internationally they are probably known in every nation. At least the concepts behind them should be.
With a functional approach a transfer of ownership concept is not needed here either. There are differences between the solutions of priority etc for different kinds of documents, and the parties choose the terms (documents) from what they like to achieve. If they want priority from the creditors just by the transfer of the document, they choose a condition to achieve this and take relevant precautions. If they prefer priority through notice to the holder of the goods they chose another term and the following precautions.
When a document of title is created and the goods are left to a third party, the transfer of the document is in principle the only way to transfer rights to the goods. However, a seller is considered to have the right of stoppage in transit even if the document has been delivered.[146]
It may also be noted that there might, according to common practice, be several documents of title for the same goods. This creates a risk of double selling and a document can therefore not be trusted completely.[147]
There are no specific rules and no clear principle concerning priority over the creditors when a third party carrier carries the good. It could however be stated that the contractual conditions concerning the right to direct the goods should govern the solution. If the seller has the right to direct the goods somewhere else than to the buyer, the buyer should not have priority over the creditors of the seller. On the other hand it could also be argued that the buyer should get priority from the moment that the goods is in the possession of the third party carrier if this third party is told who should get the goods.[148]

### 6.8.5. "Brevi manu traditio"

If the buyer already has the goods in his possession at the time of the acquisition he is protected from the seller's creditors by the agreement. The tradition

[145] Johansson, Svante O: Stoppningsrätt, 2001, p 458.
[146] Håstad 1996, p 179. Johansson, Svante O: Stoppningsrätt, 2001, p 351.
[147] Maritime Code (Sjölagen) 13:53–56.
[148] Johansson, Svante O: Stoppningsrätt, 2001, p 458–459.

requirement is, seen to be, fulfilled in advance. This is in accordance with the cutting off doctrine mentioned above (see physical tradition). The transferee gets priority from the moment the contract is closed.

### 6.8.6. "Constitutum possessorium"

It is (as mentioned several times above) in principle not possible to get priority over the creditors without the transferor being cut off from the physical possibilities to reach the movable. Constitutum possessorium cannot be used. If the parties do want to leave a tangible in possession of the transferor, it is possible to use registration instead (see 2.1.4.).

The registration procedure is prescribed for in the 1845 Bills of Sales Act. It requires the buyer to establish evidence of the sales contract in a written, certified document. The document must identify the goods. This document must be notified in a local newspaper (in the seller's home-area) together with information about the purchase price, the seller's and the buyer's names and their professions. Finally, the document together with evidence of the notification must be registered with the Enforcement Authority within eight days from the notification. It is a complicated procedure and that may partly explain why it is not used very often. The main reason during the last 20 years, has however probably been that a registration in accordance with the Bills of Sales Act does not have priority over the former floating charge.

Registration according to the Bills of Sales Act is unfortunately not a system that works well. It is not practical and there is no awareness of the system among the public.

### 6.9. Denuntiation – "tradition" for movables under third party control

There is an act from 1936 that specifically regulates notice concerning a security right that has been given in the movable.[149] Such notice could be given by the pawnor who is able to give the notice in any form, or by the pawnee who must show written evidence of the security agreement.

It is held that the said act should not be applicable to sales.[150] Notice could then be given in any form. The notice can be given either by the transferor or the transferee, in any form they want.

There is also a special rule concerning non-negotiable claims (receivables) that do not require that notice should be given in any special form. It is sufficient that notice is given.[151]

---

[149] Lag (1936:88) om pantsättning av lös egendom som innehaves av tredje man.

[150] Håstad 1996 p 230-231.

[151] Act of Promissory Notes § 31. Martinson 2002, p 278–279, 302, with the citations given there.

To get priority over the creditors of the transferor it is not considered necessary to have consent from the third party. In fact a motive behind the rule concerning notice of security right was to abolish the former order where consent was held as necessary.[152]
However, in some cases it might be necessary with the consent from the third party since a transfer might otherwise be a breach of contract between the transferor and the third party. An example is the synallagmatic contracts where it should sometimes not be possible to transfer the rights of one of the contracting parties. If the third party cannot be obliged to pay or deliver to anyone else than the original counterpart, there cannot be anything for the transferee to have priority in.[153]
If a third party keeps generic goods the transferor has an obligatory right. Since the right as such is considered to be a specialised object any transfer of this right would concern a right in rem against the transferor and his creditors. A claim for money against the third party is a mere claim when competing with the creditors of the third party, but against the creditors of the transferor the right to the claim is a right in rem.
When notice is given to the third party in these cases it could be done in any way – by the transferor or the transferee without any formal requirements.[154]

## 6.10. Registration

Priority over the creditors of the transferor could as an opt alternative to tradition be reached by registration if the transfer concerns tangibles, as said above (see 6.8.6.)[155]
Registration is also the sole possibility for priority when it comes to financial instruments, ships and aeroplanes that are regulated by special acts.[156]
The concepts "constitutive" and "declaratory" are foreign to the Swedish approach. Registration has no other effect than creating priority over the creditors and other holders of rights (other transferees).

---

[152] Lennander, Gertrud: Panthavares skyldigheter vid pantavtal om lös egendom, 1977, p 196 note 40.
[153] Martinson 2002, p 202–221, 249–264, with the citations given there.
[154] Act of Promissory Notes § 31.
[155] This type of registration is regulated in the 1845 Bills of sales Act.
[156] For financial instruments: Lag (1998:1479) om kontoföring av finansiella instrument (Act of Registration of Financial Instruments) chapter 6. Sjölagen (Maritime Code) 2:9. Aeroplanes: no registration for protection against seller's creditors! Håstad 1996, p 251f.

## 6.11. Consensual system – consensus principle

### 6.11.1. Background

To make a few remarks from a Swedish view the question when ownership or some aspects of "ownership" generally pass with the conclusion of the contract, could be interpreted as to concern – *priority over the creditors of the transferor*. As said above a consensus principle is used to determine priority in some situations – especially consumer sales and intellectual property.[157] Party autonomy is considered to be a central interest to regard (see 6.5.2.), and it could be said that party autonomy is used for different kinds of efficiency arguments in favour of a consensus solution and against a tradition requirement. The background of the consensus principle would however not so much be described with a party autonomy argument. That argument is only rarely openly used in creditor priority questions.

Historically (se above 6.8.1. physical tradition) a consensus principle was used in Sweden.[158] The tradition principle grew strong during the 20:th century and the courts used it in every situation where it was possible to either transfer physical possession or give notice to a relevant third party. Notice requirements were in that way created concerning different kinds of joint ownership and sales of the shares in such property. Eventually the common belief could be described as a general tradition (or notice) requirement in every situation where it would be possible. A consensus principle would then be limited to intellectual property and some special cases.[159] (One such special case is when the sole owner of a company makes dispositions between himself and the company.)[160]

When the consensus principle was introduced (or reintroduced) for consumer sales a year ago the motives were consumer concerns. An assumption was that the risk for fraud and evidence produced afterwards would be small.[161] The risk would probably be considered higher concerning security arrangements and sales to other than consumers such as trading partners and next of kin.

According to the proposition for the changes in the Consumers Sales Act consumers often have no knowledge of the tradition requirement. Goods that are paid for are sometimes left with the seller. Concerning e.g. white goods, furs, furniture, boats, cars, etc. it is done on a regular basis. This is valuable goods so

---

[157] It should be noted that a lot of questions concerning intellectual property and creditor priority remains to be handled. To talk about a consensus principle concerning intellectual property is therefore not a good description. In fact to use such a description could produce an order that is not thought through in all the necessary aspects. E.g. Martinson 2002, p 100-105.

[158] Göranson, Ulf: Traditionsprincipen, 1985, p 233ff.

[159] Helander, Bo: Kreditsäkerhet i lös egendom, 1984, p 304ff.

[160] NJA 2000 s 88. Martinson 2002, p 287–288, 304–306.

[161] SOU 1995:11 p 176-177.

the losses are serious for the consumers. In addition a consumer rarely has the possibility to get a security to protect his claim. The loss that the consumer suffers is not a business risk, acceptable in accordance with market economy reasons. The consumer cannot pass the loss on in a chain of transactions. To the consumer the loss must be perceived as unexpected and unfair. There are however not much statistics concerning the real losses made by consumers during the years.
This may be perceived as a less extensive argumentation than what ought to forego an important change of this kind. The change has also been foregone in doctrine.[162] A good question is however why the consensus principle was only reintroduced for consumer sales. The main answer is probably that a general change would have been too thorough. Swedish lawyers are used to the tradition principle and some defend it quite strongly. On the practical level it must also be remembered that the commission that suggested the change for consumers was formed just to overview some questions concerning consumer protection. They did therefore not have the mandate to suggest a general change.
The Consumer Sales Act and the consensus principle do only apply when the other party is a professional.

### 6.11.2. Generic goods

As outlined above (see 1.4.1. and 2.1.) it is important that a right in rem should only be against a particular individual asset. The requirements for identification have already been mentioned, 6.5.1.
To elaborate a little on the question if rights in rem can only refer to a particular, individual asset: There is an exception when money is held on account for several others but has been mixed. As long as the money has been held separate from the debtor's own accounts the principals have the right to separate the money in bankruptcy even if there is not enough to pay the total amount.[163] The principals get a dividend out of the separated amount. They are also entitled to damages and can make claims in the rest of the bankruptcy.
The said exception is made in an act that concerns accountability for money, but it is argued that the same principles should sometimes be used concerning generic goods.[164] The Supreme Court has done so concerning corn in a silo.[165] Other examples that are mentioned in doctrine are fish in a pisciculture and piglets in a pigsty.[166]

---

[162] Ulf Göranson's thesis from 1985; "Traditionsprincipen", in which the tradition principle was criticized, especially in the context of consumer sales.
[163] Act of Priority in Accounts (Redovisningsmedelslagen; Lag (1944:181) om redovisningsmedel).
[164] Walin, Gösta: Separationsrätt, 1977, p 154.
[165] NJA 1994 s 506.
[166] Håstad 1996 p 173-174.

It should be noted that the named exceptions from the principle of identification all concern goods that are separated. Even though it is not possible to tell which goods belong to a certain principal it is possible to see that the goods do not belong to the liable person who is accountable. It should also be noted that *the said exceptions concern situations where the goods have not originally been owned by the person who is later accountable.* It would therefore not be possible for a buyer or a pawnee to claim these exceptions if the goods stays with the seller or pawnor.

### 6.11.3. Future goods

From a Supreme Court ruling (NJA 1973 s 635) concerning a certain kind of future receivables it has been argued that a contract, concerning future goods, will give the transferee priority over the creditors from the moment the goods have come into existence and the different tradition requirements have been met. In the Supreme Court decision the buyer of some transports (debtor of the receivable) had been given notice before the transports where made. If such a principle were to be used on cases where the consensus principle would apply, it would be sufficient to identify the good with for example marking. A contract could in other words be closed in advance for "future goods".

This kind of argumentation is however dangerous. What it does is to create a legal object out of traditional legal structures. Such a creation generates consequential beliefs that are often not thought through. It is necessary to be careful and weigh the different interests in the very different situations that could come into question.[167]

Since the consensus principle mainly applies to consumer sales it can here be mentioned that it does not seem to be very problematical to create a possibility for consumers to get priority for future goods. If a consumer has ordered a standardized boat that the seller has to build, the interests of the creditors would not be very much put aside if the consumer should get the boat when it has come into existence. There has yet been little discussion about future and manufactured goods. The Law Commission was of the opinion that it should be sufficient that the production of the ordered goods has started.[168]

A more problematical solution is if the consumer would get a priority of the meaning that the bankruptcy estate would be obliged to build the rest of the boat. Such a solution would for example make it harder to wind up a bankruptcy.

---

[167] Martinson 2002, p 206–222, 350–381.
[168] SOU 1995:11 p 168.

### 6.11.4. Sale of goods not (yet) owned by the transferor[169]

Such a sale would probably give priority to the consumer if the goods were still in the possession of the deliverer. Through the contract between the seller and the deliverer the good is individualised and, in a way, marked for the consumer. However if the seller has not paid the deliverer the goods will not be delivered.

### 6.11.5. Contract subject to a suspensive condition;

If the goods are marked for the consumer he will probably get priority as long as it has not been made clear that the condition is not met.

### 6.11.6. Alternative obligations

The effects of alternative obligations could be relevant both when a consensus principle applies and under a tradition principle. The alternative goods can be in the possession of the transferee and in such cases the question of alternative obligations are comparable. (It is however hard to find this specific question discussed in Swedish doctrine.)

If a buyer has bought either a certain blue boat or a certain yellow car and it is up to the seller to decide which, it could be argued that the seller has too much discretion. The result would probably be that the buyer would not be protected A situation where the transferor has the right to decide how the obligation should be fulfilled can be hard to separate from a sale of a generic good. The parties could agree that the seller could fulfil the agreement with one out of a hundred specified cars, and the agreement would then be close to an agreement where the seller can deliver any car that meets the requirements. The hundred cars could be all the cars that the seller has got.

What has been said about the seller's discretion could also be said about a contract where instead the transferee has the right to decide which one of several specified objects that he wants. It is the same problem to draw a line between sale of a generic good and sale of a specific good. However, if the seller is obliged to let the buyer have a real choice between all of the specified objects, the seller cannot make dispositions with any one of the objects. That could be argued to be a conclusive difference against the case where the seller decides.

---

[169] One could argue that the asset could not be individualised and marked through the seller and its predecessor (as mentioned in the second sentence above), if this contract is for generic goods. However, one could maybe argue some kind of co-ownership (or co-preferential right) in the bulk of generic goods.

6.11.7. Statistic assumptions – consensus or tradition?

Consumer sales are probably the most common kind of contract in Sweden and the consensus principle could therefore be described as the main rule in practice. However as said before, the consumer sale is the only kind of transaction, apart from sales of intellectual property, where the consensus principle applies.[170]

6.12. Real agreement

There is no such thing as a real agreement and nothing that comes close to such a concept. In fact it is a very foreign concept for a Swedish lawyer. A "declaration or agreement separate from the underlying obligation" is not understandable from a Swedish perspective. When we decide that there is an obligation the obligation itself is enough to bind the parties and to have effect against other parties. If there are additional agreements they are seen as adjustments or a complements to the first ground for the obligation. The fact that the tradition requirements also most often have to be met to give priority against creditors is seen as something else. – In other words there are no differences concerning the effects against third parties between obligations that stem from different grounds.

6.13. Payment

Although an ownership concept is not used, the notion of payment having effects on the buyer's possibilities is relevant in Sweden. When the buyer has bought something under the condition that the seller has the right to take the good back if it is not paid ("retention of title") the buyer are under a penal obligation not to sell, pawn or otherwise dispose of the good.[171] As long as the good is not paid the buyer's creditors must also first pay the seller before they can demand the enforcement service to sell the good for their credits.[172] The motives for these respective rules are to protect the seller and to promote trade.[173]

## 7. Double selling – double disposals

The question who acquires ownership after a double selling could in Sweden as well be put as – who wins? A clear general principle is that the first transferee (B)

[170] And also, as mentioned, negotiable instruments sold by financial institutions, Promissory Notes Act § 22.
[171] The Penal Code (Brottsbalken) 10:4.
[172] Enforcement Code (Utsökningsbalken) 9:10.
[173] Håstad 1996, p 182.

wins as long as the latter (C) has not acquired possession, or equivalent, in good faith.[174]
However, concerning tangibles B has the right to pay C, what he paid or the market price, and in that way get the movable. B:s right to redemption must be used in six months after B was made aware about C:s right and possession.
The general principle would be that C should not have suspected that someone had bought the movable or in other words that the movable had already been sold. The wording does however differ in the different acts and articles. In the Act of Good Faith Acquisitions that concerns tangibles the wording is more or less the same as in the mentioned general principle.[175] Concerning negotiable instruments the wording in the Promissory Notes Act is "without that he knew or did set aside the caution that he reasonably should have taken". The rule for double sale of receivables (bona fide acquisition of receivables only possible in double sale situations) just states "good faith".[176]
The good faith requirement for negotiable instruments is not very strict, but it should not be interpreted as to take "gross negligence" for a buyer not to be in good faith. The degree of good faith required by the buyer is higher than that in order not to relax the buyer's duty of scrutiny too much. The good faith requirement for receivables is stricter than that for negotiable instruments, due to the fact that these are not designated for market transactions.[177]
It has been argued by some that it should not matter if C is in bad faith if A decides to sell and delivers the good to him instead.[178] This has however not (yet) had any impact of importance.

## 8. Selling in a chain

Selling in a chain is for example when A sells to B and B to C, and A delivers the property directly to C. With a substantial perspective a question to be asked is ownership directly transferred from A to C or is B said to have obtained ownership for a "logical second". That is not a question at all with a functional approach. Sales in a chain are not considered to be different than other sales. The respective parties are bound against each other as in any contractual relationship. A and C have in principle nothing to do with each other. (There is however one kind of speciality concerning sales in a chain, but that concerns taxation and

---

174 The Act of Good faith Acquisition (Godtrosförvärslagen) § 2. Promissory Notes Act 14 §, 31 §.
175 The Act of Good faith Acquisition (Godtrosförvärslagen) § 2.
176 § 14 respectively § 31 of the Promissory Notes Act.
177 Walin, Gösta, Lagen om skuldebrev m.m. (a comment to the Act of Promissory Notes), 1997, p. 121.
178 Håstad 1996 p 83–84.

registration. If B sells land to C on the exact same terms as B bought the land from A, B does not have to pay the land registration fee.)

If the goods are delivered directly to C, C will get priority against the creditors of B. At the same time B will get priority over the creditors of A.

The question of sales in a chain might however also concern sales on account for others – commission. Some of the effects from sales through commission are sometimes described with the simplification that ownership passes directly from A to C. What this description underlines is that the creditors of B in principle are unable to reach the goods or the proceeds from the sales of it. A is safe as long as B keeps the goods and the proceeds separated from his own belongings.[179]

If the *contract A–B* is invalid this invalidity could not necessarily be claimed by A. C could have made a good faith acquisition (according to both the Act of Good Faith Acquisition and the Act of Commission). A does then loose his possibilities to claim the goods, but if it is a tangible A has the right to pay C, what he paid or the market price, and in that way get the goods.

It could also be argued that A should have the right to separate in bankruptcy the payment that B did get, or alternatively the unpaid claim. Such a solution would however be questioned indeed. The discussion concerning separability is rather open.[180]

If the *contract B–C* is invalid this is a matter that concerns these two parties. A can in principle not do anything about it.

The circumstances could however be that A has an interest in the second sale in such a way that the second sale simply has to be considered to be a contractual condition. Under these circumstances A can terminate the contract with B if B:s contract with C is invalid. A could in other words get the goods back if B brakes his contract with A by being a part of an invalid contract with C.

When the sale B–C is done on commission the invalidity of the contract B–C will have the effect that the "ownership goes back" to A. Commission is of course a sale on account for A and A should therefore be able to claim the goods back if it is not yet sold. B should also have the right to dispose of the goods by giving it back to A.

---

179 Håstad 1996 p 234-245.

180 Håstad 1996 p 164 ff. Walin, Gösta: Separationsrätt, 1977, p 185 ff.

## 9. Consequences of insolvency

### 9.1. General issues

#### 9.1.1. Termination of contracts

During a formal bankruptcy the debtor looses his right to make decisions concerning his property and his debts.[181] (The Bankruptcy Code is formally applicable to both businesses and private persons but private persons are more seldom put into bankruptcy since it is often impractical and expensive.) The administrator has, as a representative for the creditors and the debtor, the right to terminate contracts. In fact a better description is probably that contracts are terminated through the bankruptcy if the administrator does not demand that a contract is fulfilled. The administrator has the right to make such a demand only if the contract is not of a personal kind, in other words of a kind where it does not matter that the debtor does not fulfil his obligations personally. It is also necessary that the administrator can pay or put up a secured guarantee for the obligations of the debtor. Otherwise the counterpart has the right to stay out of the contract.[182] When a contract is terminated the counterpart must claim his rights in the bankruptcy, i.e. get his rights in rem and the bankruptcy dividend for his claims.
If the insolvency proceedings take the form of a formal (decided by the court) business reconstruction, instead of a bankruptcy, the debtor does not loose his capacity to decide, but the reconstruction will probably not succeed if he does not do as the administrator says. Contracts are not terminated through the reconstruction decision, but the aim of the reconstruction is to negotiate new conditions with the counterparts. If a counterpart cannot agree upon the terms that the administrator suggests, the debtor will in principle not fulfil the contract. The counterpart must instead claim damages. These damages might be reduced to as low as 25 % if there is a qualified majority of the creditors that accepts the total reconstruction plan. If the counterpart has security he can use the security as long at it suffices.[183]

#### 9.1.2. Generic goods – specific goods[184]

When a seller (donor or pawnor etc) goes bankrupt and the buyer has *not taken possession* the seller's bankruptcy administrator would say that the tradition

---

[181] Bankruptcy Code (Konkurslagen) 3:1.
[182] Sales of Goods Act (Köplagen) § 63. Håstad 1996 p 402 ff.
[183] Business Reconstruction Act – Företagsrekonstruktionslagen; Lag (1996:764) om företagsrekonstruktion. Folkesson, Enar: Företaget i ekonomisk kris, 2002, p 122ff.
[184] See also above especially section 6.5.1.

requirements have not been fulfilled. The buyer would have to come to a new agreement with the administrator, and this is often something that the administrator wants since the estate has to be sold. It is normally more costly to find a new buyer.
When the buyer *has taken the goods into his possession* it is typically specified – at least in regards to the sellers other goods. The buyer gets priority over the seller's creditors as long as the contract is not void or possible to recover. In such cases the administrator would get the goods back. If the contract, or the buyer's lack of performance, gives the seller the right to terminate or revoke the contract, the bankruptcy administrator could also use this right.
If it is the buyer (pawnee etc) that goes bankrupt and the goods are *not delivered* the bankruptcy administrator will terminate the contract and not deliver.
When the goods *have already been delivered* a seller is required to have a retention of title clause to keep any possibilities to get the goods back – to keep his right in rem. Otherwise he will only get a dividend for his claim. If the contract were void or possible to terminate on other grounds than lack of performance from the buyer the seller would get the goods back as long as it is specified. When the goods are generic the seller will either get a general dividend, or, if the buyer has bought from several sellers and the kind of goods in question are separated from his own, a dividend out of the separated goods. In some cases there the buyer has mixed the goods with his own, it has been seen as unreasonable not to give the seller a right in rem and it has therefore been granted. An example is that a counterfeit or a thief has got his hands on something shortly before he goes bankrupt. In theory this is a somewhat problematical field in the Swedish system (and it would be an interesting subject to do more research in).
Of importance in this context is also that the administrator can claim a right to enter into a contract (konkursbos inträdesrätt) that he thinks is good for the creditors. As long as the performance that the estate must deliver is independent of the performer's qualities, such as a delivery of goods or a payment normally is, the counterpart has to accept the estate as a new partner. From this it follows that it would not be possible for the administrator to enter into a contract where the performance is dependant of the performer.

### 9.1.3. Avoidance, recovery, actio Pauliana

There are possibilities to recover (avoid) contracts that are especially damaging for the creditors. The formal requirements can be summarized as 1) there must be a formal bankruptcy or business reconstruction proceeding, 2) the contract or the act to be recovered must have been a disadvantage to the creditors, and, 3) the contract or the act to be recovered must have taken place within a certain time before the application for the insolvency proceeding, the time limit vary for different circumstances.

The rules for recovery are to be found in the fourth chapter of the Bankruptcy Code. There is a general clause for unfair transactions.[185] To use this rule it must be proven that the debtor had intent to favour someone or damage a creditor. The act to be recovered must also have contributed to the insolvency. If the act is directed towards a close relative there is no time limit and in other cases the time limit is five years.

In addition to the mentioned general clause according to which intent is considered relevant, there are also several objective rules. One of these concerns beneficiary transfers, as mentioned above (see 6.3.). Beneficiary transactions and other non-businesslike transactions can be recovered (annulled) within six months. If the transaction has been done within six months and a year the beneficiary can escape if he can show that the debtor evidently had more belongings than he had debts at the time of the gift. The one-year time limit is extended to three years when the recovery claim is directed towards close relatives.[186]

Salaries, pensions and such can be recovered within a six months limit to the extent that they obviously exceed what could be regarded as reasonable having regard to the work performed, the profitability of the operation and the circumstances in general.[187] Extended time limits apply under the same circumstances as for beneficiary transaction. The salary rule is typically used for small companies where the owners pay themselves large salaries when they know that the firm will go bankrupt.

The two major objective rules concerns payment of debts and transfer of security for unsecured debt. If such transactions are not ordinary they can be recovered if they have been made within three months before the application for insolvency proceedings. If the receiver is a close relative the time limit is two years, as long as the relative does not show that the transaction did not contribute to the insolvency.[188]

185 Bankruptcy Code (Konkurslagen) 4:5. Lennander, Gertrud: Återvinning i konkurs, 1994, p 127ff.

186 Bankruptcy Code (Konkurslagen) 4:6. Lennander, Gertrud: Återvinning i konkurs, 1994, p 172ff.

187 Bankruptcy Code (Konkurslagen) 4:8. Lennander, Gertrud: Återvinning i konkurs, 1994, p 187-188.

188 Bankruptcy Code (Konkurslagen) 4:10 and 4:12. Lennander, Gertrud: Återvinning i konkurs, 1994, p 189ff.

## 9.2. Insolvency of the transferor

### 9.2.1. The acquirer's protection against the transferor's general creditors

As said (see sections 1.4.1.2., 6.2.4. and 6.8.) the acquirer generally must fulfil the requirements that the tradition principle brings (transfer of possession, notice or registration). The central concern has often been to protect creditors from fraud and evidence constructed afterwards.
A consensus principle (protection from the moment of conclusion of the contract) is used mainly for consumer sales and intellectual property (see 6.11.).

### 9.2.2. Specific goods – generic goods

The tradition requirements are applicable to both specific and generic goods. Through the transfer of possession, the notice, or the registration, the goods are specified.
For consumer sales, where the consensus principle is applicable, the same rule is used for both specific and generic goods. The problems with identification have been described above (see 6.11.).

### 9.2.3. Future goods

As said above (see 6.11.3. future goods): The different tradition requirements could, depending on the circumstances, be made in advance, before the goods have come into "existence". Such solutions must however always be thoroughly thought through. It is necessary to be careful and weigh the different interests in the very different situations that could come into question.[189]
If a consumer orders something to be manufactured it can be argued that the consumer should be protected from the moment that the production of the ordered goods have started. Since the rule for consumer sales is new there has not yet been much discussion about these problems.[190]

### 9.2.4. Goods not yet delivered to the transferor – sales in a chain

If the insolvent transferor has bought the good from a previous seller and has either paid it or taken possession of it without retention of title condition from the seller, the seller cannot get it back. The acquirer can then if he is a *consumer* be

---

[189] Martinson 2002, p 73–74, 100–105, and for the example of receivables p 206–221, 350–381, 411–416, 630–632.
[190] As said, see 5.6, it is in the prepatory works, SOU 1995:11 p 168, just said that it should be sufficient that the production of the ordered goods have started.

protected through specification. Goods that are ordered especially for the consumer would probably be considered as marked for the consumer through a bookkeeping note.[191]

If the goods are generic in the possession of the seller (and the seller has been paid so he must deliver) it could be argued that the consumer could be protected anyhow. The goods are specified since it is a part of a specific delivery, from a specific seller.[192]

If the goods have not left the seller who has not been paid, the seller can, as any seller, stop his delivery and terminate the contract.[193]

When the buyer is *not a consumer* he must normally fulfil the tradition requirements and would therefore not be protected. Under certain conditions where the insolvent transferor has the role of a "middle man" acting on account for the buyer, the acquirer will however be protected as long as the goods are identifiable.[194]

Another case occurs when the goods have not left the seller though the seller has been paid. It could then under certain circumstances be argued that the seller has been noticed and holds the goods for the acquirer, who should accordingly be protected. This solution is however not very much discussed.[195] It is probably very unusual that the transferor has paid the seller.

### 9.2.5. Different kinds of obligations

It is described as an important advantage that the same requirement, tradition, is used for all kinds of obligations. With such a solution it is often not necessary to decide if a contract is the one or the other, for example a sales or a security contract. There are however differences where the distinction between different types of contracts is in different ways determinate for the protection against the creditors.

As mentioned (see 6.3., 6.6.2. and 9.1.3.) there are special rules for beneficiary obligations that have the effect of protecting both the donor and his creditors. For example a donation can be recalled if the donor gets in economic trouble as long as the movable is not handed over. Beneficiary transactions and other non-business transactions are also subject to recovery.

---

[191] Compare SOU 1995:11, Proposition 2001/02:134.

[192] Compare SOU 1995:11, Proposition 2001/02:134.

[193] Sales of Goods Act (Köplagen) § 61.

[194] Håstad 1996 p 145-147.

[195] The normative support for this is the same as for the principle that notice to a third party holder of the goods are sufficient. Compare Håstad 1996 p 230.

### 9.2.6. Obligation to re-transfer – on the ground of termination or invalidity

A contract might be terminated after delivery of the goods. If the ground for termination is lack of payment from the transferee (buyer) it would with a functional approach be dealt with as a problem of the transferor's protection from insolvency of the transferee – in other words a less abstract level than the concept to separate the re-transfer from its origin leads us to.[196] The problems of insolvency of the transferee are discussed in section 9.3. The principles mentioned there are: 1) To get the goods back on the grounds of lack of payment the seller need a retention of title clause. He can then separate the goods from the bankruptcy estate, provided that the goods have not been mixed with the first transferee's property and thus have lost their individuality. If retention of title has not been made the transferee can never take the goods back from the bankruptcy estate, he can only make a dividend claim in the bankruptcy. 2) If the ground for termination is something else than lack of payment or the contract is void, it would be possible to argue priority over the creditors. There is a Supreme Court decision that gave the seller right to get iron back since it was delivered to the buyer under false presumptions.[197] It is however a good question to what length this principle could be used – as said in 6.2.9. this is somewhat problematic field or at least not very much elaborated, see also 9.3.4.

However, what should be dealt with in this section under this heading, should from a functional approach rather be, the transferee's (buyer's) protection from the insolvency of the transferor (seller).

If the contract is terminated before delivery the buyer should not have the goods and will therefore not be given priority concerning the goods. In case the buyer has paid in advance he will only have a claim to get the money back and that claim would not be given priority. The same solution would be the result when the contract is declared void. Who is responsible and what is the cause for invalidity would generally not matter, compare below and section 9.3.4.

The contract could also be terminated after delivery of the goods. A common cause would be that the goods are defect. The buyer is then typically entitled to damages and to have his money back. Since the seller is bankrupt the claim will

---

[196] The question asked for this heading was: There has been a contract (e.g. of sale) and the movable has been transferred to the buyer. Now this contract is terminated (especially on account of non payment) and this termination creates a new obligation between the parties, i.e. an obligation to re-transfer the movable to the previous seller. The question is whether also such an obligation to re-transfer protects the (re-)acquirer (i.e. the previous seller) against the creditors of the transferor (the former buyer) from the moment of its creation. In other words: If there is a protection of the acquirer against the transferor's general creditors in cases of a sale ("consensual system"), is there a parallel also in cases where the obligation is not a contract, but e.g. unjust enrichment (or whatever such an obligation to re-transfer would be based on in the relevant legal system).

[197] NJA 1985 s 178.

only result in a dividend. If the buyer is not satisfied with the dividend he can use the goods as a security – it might have some value even if it is not good enough for the buyer. The question is however not very much discussed. In practice the problems will probably be solved without a formal cancellation of the contract. The buyer just claims the damages and keeps the goods.
If the ground for re-transfer is invalidity, the principle in non-insolvency cases is to re-transfer the goods against the re-payment of the price. When the seller is insolvent the buyer would probably still have the right to get re-payment in full. At least that would be a solution when the seller or a third party is responsible for the invalidity, compare next section.

### 9.2.7. Delictual obligations

If the buyer is responsible for the invalidity, through acts like blackmail, fraud or usury, the buyer would probably have to give the goods back with just a dividend claim. There would probably also be made a set off between the sellers claim for damages from the named crimes, and the claim of re-payment. Once again it can however be noted that this is not a much-elaborated theme in the Swedish legal doctrine.

### 9.2.8. Call options and put options

As said (see 1.4.1.2.) the tradition requirements must be fulfilled also when it comes to optional obligations. If tradition is made in advance the receiver will get priority from the moment the condition is fulfilled. This would probably not be handled differently for consumers. The consensual principle does only apply to completed sales according to the Consumer Sales Act.

### 9.2.9. Bequest by last will

If the estate of the deceased is bankrupt all belongings will be sold for the creditors. The debts must in principle be paid before anyone can get anything from the estate. If the acquirer has the goods in his possession by the time of death he has to give the goods to the estate, even if there is a will in his favour.[198] As long as the estate has not paid all the debts of the deceased it is possible for the creditors to claim back everything that has been given to the heirs.
If an estate pays all the creditors of the deceased but for some time keeps parts of the estate without dividing it, the estate might go bankrupt from debts that the estate has incurred. In such a bankruptcy an heir would not be obliged to return his inheritance. The general rules for recovery would however be applicable.

---

[198] Code of Inheritance (Ärvdabalken) Chapter 21.

### 9.2.10. Natural obligation[199]

A natural obligation to do something else than to deliver specific or generic good, would not be considered to be a right in rem. Obligations to do work can not get priority against the creditors. When the transferor can or does not fulfil his natural obligations they are transformed into claims for damages for breach of contract. These claims do not get priority as long as they are not secured by a pledge or a lien.

The term natural obligation could also be used for an already prescribed obligation. If a transferor fulfils a prescribed obligation it is possible for the transferee to get protection from the transferor's creditors in accordance with regular property law rules. The payment is considered valid and as long as there are no grounds for recovery, such as that the transferor wanted to favour the transferee on his creditors accounts, the payment would give priority.

### 9.2.11. Decision of a judge or other public authority

As said (see 6.6.4.) court orders about transfer of ownership normally concerns forfeiture in connection to criminal acts. Since a person who is convicted of a crime often has to pay compensation to injured parties, it is probably not unusual that the criminal is insolvent. A forfeiture of goods could therefore often be in conflict with the interests of the creditors. Since a forfeiture is most often decided when an authority has already taken the goods in possession it could be argued that the forfeiture should have priority through the fulfilment of the tradition requirement. However, the real motive for such a priority is rather that the goods are closely connected to crime. It would not be a good idea if for example the customs would have to give smuggled liquor to the administrator of the bankruptcy.

### 9.2.12. Acquisition through an indirect agent who goes bankrupt

If someone acquires through an indirect agent who goes bankrupt before having delivered the asset to the acquirer: Is the acquirer entitled against the agent's creditors; is he also entitled against the third party?

As mentioned in connection to the question of previous sellers, the acquirer will be protected as long as the goods are identifiable when the transferor acts on account for the buyer.

---

[199] In many jurisdictions, this term is used for obligations that can not be enforced (before court), but can be discharged (if the debtor "voluntarily" or by mistake decides to do so). In Austrian law and other jurisdictions, e.g. already prescribed obligations or obligations only invalid on account of defects of form requirements would be such "natural obligations".

The relationship between the buyer and the third party is dependant on the status given to the indirect agent. If the agent is acting on commission the acquirer has the right to take over the contractual rights and obligations from the agent. So, when the goods are not yet delivered to the agent, it is an easy solution for the principal to request that the goods are delivered directly to him against the obligation to pay.[200] It could however be argued that a difference should be made between specific and generic goods.[201]

### 9.2.13. Party autonomy

The parties have to fulfil the requirements for priority. They can however construct their dealings in different ways to achieve different advantages.
If e.g. a contractual condition according to which the acquirer should have priority against the creditors from a certain moment *after* the tradition requirements has been fulfilled would be used, such a condition would have effect. It is not a disadvantage for the creditors.

### 9.2.14. Suspensive conditions

As said (see 1.4.1.2. and above concerning options) the tradition requirements must be fulfilled also when it comes to optional obligations. If tradition is made in advance the receiver will get priority from the moment the condition is fulfilled.

## 9.3. Insolvency of the transferee

### 9.3.1. General rules

As remarked (see 6.7.1.) if the party is not solvent or gets insolvent after the contract is closed but before the movable is transferred, the contract can be annulled (terminated). The seller does not have to deliver the movable and also has the right to get the movable back from an independent deliverer, (right of stoppage in transit).
When the goods are delivered the seller looses the right to the goods and can only claim payment. The seller can however reserve title (retention of title). This is done through a contractual condition and does not have to be registered. It is generally agreed that such a condition must be made before delivery.[202]

---

[200] Commission Act (Kommissionslagen; Lag (1914:45) om kommission), 53 §, 56 §, 58 §. Håstad 1996 p 234-237.
[201] Håstad 1996 p 236-237.
[202] E.g. Adlercreutz, Axel: Finansieringsformers rättsliga reglering, 2001, p 53-54. Håstad 1996, p 185.

Compared to some other European systems the Swedish retention of title institute is rather limited. It is argued that retention of title can only be accepted for goods that are identifiable and not supposed to be consumed or sold by the buyer. A 'retention of title clause` would therefore have effect on a sale of a car, but not on sales of building material and food. Retention of title could neither be used for stock goods if it is sold to a retailer or someone else who will sell it on their own account.[203] (See 13.)

9.3.2. Termination by the seller

If the buyer is not solvent or gets insolvent after the contract is closed but *before the movable is transferred*, the contract can be annulled (terminated). It is sufficient that the seller has strong indications to believe that the buyer will not be able to pay or in other ways not fulfil his obligations under the contract. The seller will also be entitled to damages for breach of contract.

When the seller has strong indications to believe that the buyer will not be able to pay or in other ways breach the contract, he does not have to deliver the movable and also has the right to get the movable back from an independent deliverer, (right of stoppage in transit). The precise moment of delivery could be described as the moment when the buyer gets the good in his possession.[204]

Termination on other grounds than risk for non-payment is probably not very common, especially not in combination with insolvency of the transferee. The subject is not much dealt with. If the contract is terminated on another ground before delivery, there would however not be any problem concerning the protection of the seller. The seller keeps the goods.

As said, when the *goods have been delivered* the seller can claim the goods back as long as he has used a retention of title and the goods are specified. The seller does in this way have priority over the creditors already from the closing of the contract.

Termination after delivery on other grounds than lack of payment would probably give the seller priority as long as the goods are specified. This is however not a common question.

Another related question concerns delivery after the courts decision on bankruptcy. The seller is protected if he delivers, or in other words gives the buyer possession to, the goods after the bankruptcy decision or the application for business reconstruction.[205] In these situations the administrator must either comply with a claim to send the goods back or pay the goods. The principle could

[203] E.g. Adlercreutz, Axel: Finansieringsformers rättsliga reglering, 2001, p 65. Håstad 1996, p 189ff.

[204] Johansson Svante O: Stoppningsrätt, p 200.

[205] Sales of Goods Act (Köplagen) § 63.

be described with a fence metaphor. When the decision of bankruptcy or filing for business reconstruction is made, the property is put under the control of the administrator. His role is to keep every new delivery outside. If he wants some of it he must be prepared to pay in full with the money of the estate.
It is also mentioned in the Sales of Goods Act that the administrator as an alternative can give the seller a security.[206] (This is however often not possible in practice since an insolvent estate seldom has security to put up.)

### 9.3.3. Termination by the buyer

If the seller has delivered the goods on credit when the buyer goes bankrupt, the seller will only have a dividend claim in the bankruptcy (provided that there is no retention of title). Thus, there is in most cases no reason for the buyer to terminate the contract in this situation. But if the buyer does terminate it, the goods must be returned. The question does not seem to have been dealt with in Swedish law.
If the goods have been delivered on credit after the outbreak of the bankruptcy, the seller may demand the goods back (according to 63 § in the Sales Act – see the fence metaphor). The buyer's termination of the contract does not imply anything else.

### 9.3.4. Invalidity of the contract[207]

If the transferee is responsible for the invalidity it could give the seller a better position. In the case NJA 1985 s 187 a retention of title was not made, but the Supreme Court gave the seller right to get the goods back because of void, (see 6.2.9. and 9.2.6.).
Other cases concerning the combination of insolvency and invalidity, is not a common theme in Sweden.[208] What will be described in the following are some simple outlines concerning possible ways to argue.
When the buyer is responsible for the invalidity and it is discovered before the goods have been delivered, the seller will of course not deliver; especially not if the buyer is insolvent. If the invalidity is discovered after the delivery, the principle above, in NJA 1985 s 187, might be used.
If the transferor is responsible for the invalidity and the transferee still wants to keep the agreement, the invalidity would not be a ground for protection of the transferor. The invalidity will so to speak not be relevant before the transferee

---

[206] Sales of Goods Act (Köplagen) § 63.
[207] Cf. PECL Ch. 4 and 15.
[208] See however Walin, Gösta; Separationsrätt 1977, p 61 and the aspects dealt with by Göransson, Ulf; Ogiltighet i sakrätten – svag ogiltighets genomslagskraft mot medkontrahents singularssuccessor, 1984.

claims the contract to be void. (This might again be something that is explained by the functional approach – there is so to speak no problem to consider before someone who is entitled to say so, says it.) When the transferee is bankrupt and the goods is delivered, it is likely that the transferee does not use the invalidity since the estate would not have to pay more than the dividend to keep the goods. (In fact the transferor should in principle rather be obliged to pay damages to the transferee for not having the deal as he expected, but that sum would be set off against the claim for the prize.) The transferor should in other words not be able to avoid the contract on the ground of invalidity. He would instead have to use the common ground that the transferee cannot pay. The seller's protection in this respect has already been described, see 9.3.2. If the goods are delivered a valid retention of title is necessary.

Invalidities are of different kinds and it might be to say too much to here declare general solutions. What has just been said about invalidities that the transferor is responsible for, would be limited to more grave misconduct of the transferor, such as threat, fraud and usury. However not all grounds for invalidity fall in that category. The invalidity might also be neutral, such as if one of the parties has not fulfilled the formalities for the contract in question. In case the invalidity is neutral both parties should be able to use the invalidity. The transferor would therefore be able to use this as a ground for avoiding the contract. This would probably be the case even if the goods are delivered and the transferee goes bankrupt. The principle above, in NJA 1985 s 187, might be used.

If the ground for invalidity stems from a third party, the contract might be valid anyway. A third party could for example blackmail someone to enter into an agreement with another party who is in good faith. The contract can in such a case be valid.[209] When the contract is not valid because the counterpart should have known about the third party's influence, the same arguments that have been outlined above could be used. A transferor who has used the third party's influence should in principle not be able to claim that ground to protect himself. If the ground for invalidity is more neutral he would however be able to do that, and it would probably give him priority in bankruptcy.

### 9.4. Original acquisition

An original acquisition could have the effect that the seller is not protected and not given priority in the buyer's bankruptcy. If the buyer mixes the property with his own the seller will have just a claim for damages in the buyer's bankruptcy. In case the buyer sells the property to someone who makes a good faith acquisition the seller will also be given just a claim for damages in the buyer's bankruptcy.

---

209 (Act of Contract) – Lag om avtal och andra rättshandlingar på förmögenhetsrättens område, (1915:218), § 29-31.

However, if the money the buyer got from his sale is identifiable, it could however be argued that the seller should be given priority to the money.
If the buyer is a company the seller will also be protected by a right to claim the physical person who made the sale for the buyer. That person has typically committed a crime and is therefore personally responsible for damages.

## Part III: Original acquisition

### 10. Acquisition through attachment, mixture or processing

It is possible for the acquirer to make the transferor loose his right in rem. Since a movable must be identifiable to uphold a right in rem the transferor will loose his rights if the good is mixed or combined with other property (irrevocable attachment to a dominant movable, *accessio,* or mixture of movables, *confusio* and *commixtio*). The transferor will instead get a claim for damages. It is in principle also a crime to mix or combine goods in such a way that a transferor looses his right.
Under some circumstances it is argued that the transferor can get a right to a share of the total of goods that his good has been mixed or combined with. One such case is if the acquirer has not mixed or combined the good with his own property. Another case is when the combined goods are at the same level; that is equally important and expensive. The question is discussed, but a clear doctrine has not been elaborated.[210]
It could be stressed that the solutions will probably differ between retention of title cases and other cases as stolen, lent and rented property. In retention of title cases the interest of the sellers is considered to be very different and only concern payment. Therefore they should not be given priority except in situations where it is easy and cost efficient to take the goods back. An example that illustrates how the sellers' interest is treated, is the lorry tyre case. The Supreme Court decided that the tyres should not be possible to take back after they had been mounted on the lorry.[211] It might here also been important that tyres are a consumption goods. If it instead had been a stolen car stereo that had been combined with the thief's car, the outcome would probably be different.
Another case is processing of goods (*specificatio*). According to the textbook solution the processor could get a better right to the processed goods if the value of the goods is much increased. The textbook example is the artist who paints on a piece of wood that belongs to someone else. In such a case the artist has to pay for the piece of wood, but he gets a better right (ownership) to it.

### 11. Acquisitions in good faith

With the functional approach good faith acquisitions concerns only the question if the subject with the oldest right, A, gets the property back or not. The term

---

210 Håstad 1996, p 168ff. Walin, Gösta: Separationsrätt, 1977, p 88.
211 NJA 1960 s 9. Compare Håstad p 188 who declares the opinion that the precedent should be limited since the car was sold.

ownership is avoided and the term actually used is "better right". The court will decide that A or C has the "better right" to the property, not that one of them has ownership. The decision to give A the better right does not decide the question between A and X, if X turns up and claims a better right. As a consequence A could be given "better right", but not be responsible for damages that the property has caused.

### 11.1. Field of application

There are several rules concerning bona fide purchases or acquisitions in good faith. For tangibles the principles from old doctrine and practice was manifested through the 1986 Act of Good Faith Acquisition. Negotiable instruments and non-negotiable claims (receivables) are regulated trough the 1936 Act of Promissory Notes. There are also good faith acquisition rules in the Act of Financial Instruments and in a few more acts of various kinds. (And also for land and real estate.) The main principles are the same in all these acts, though the details vary. Generally there is no difference between ownership and security right.
In the following the rules for tangibles, negotiable instruments and claims (receivables) will be dealt with. What is said about sale is applicable also to security rights. Usufructuary rights are excluded since the theme here concerns "purchase" and there are some differences between bona fide acquisitions of usufructuary rights and so called strong rights in rem as ownership and security rights. (In short it could be argued that the owner should be able to decide to whom he wants to let the property, and then be liable for possible breaches of contract that such a decision might lead to. Compare section 2.1.2.)

#### 11.1.1. Seller has never been the owner

It is possible to make a good faith acquisition of *tangibles* even if the seller has never been the owner. It is sufficient that the seller has possession and transfers this possession to the acquirer who is in good faith at the time of delivery.
For a long time there were no difference made between different sellers. From 1 July 2003 this has however been changed.[212] It is decided that a difference should be made between sellers who got possession to the goods through possession breaking crimes as theft or robbery and sellers who got possession through other ways as lease, lending, deceit, usury etc. The rightful owner may nowadays claim the goods within six months if the purchase in good faith was made from a thief or a robber. There is however a definitive 10-year limit. (The former order has been discussed numerous times since some consider it to be the most efficient order and some view it as a totally unreasonable solution. This debate has often

[212] SFS 2003:161 concerning changes in the Act of Good Faith Acquisition.

occurred in media. It has also been a popular theme for some members of parliament to use for official suggestions to change the law. The order of good faith acquisition has been the target for several governmental reports during the last fifty years.)

If a good faith acquisition is made the rightful owner has the right to redeem the good, (see also section 6.). The rightful, or in other words the first, owner, A, has the right to pay C, what he paid or the market price, and in that way get the movable. Since A can insure himself against several kinds of losses of the goods, A can be rather sure to get the goods back with the help of the insurance money. A:s right to redemption must be used within six months after A was made aware about C:s right and possession.

For *negotiable instruments* (negotiable promissory notes) the possibilities for good faith acquisitions are wider than for tangibles. There is no difference between different kinds of sellers and it is therefore possible to make a good faith acquisition from the thief. [213] The rightful owner does not have any right of redemption. He can only claim the thief or whoever managed to get the negotiable instrument from him.

There are different kinds of negotiable instruments with different possibilities in regards to good faith acquisitions. If the promissory note is to be paid to the holder of the document there is almost no burden on the buyer to investigate if the seller is the rightful owner. For promissory notes that are to be paid to a specific person or to whoever he transfers the note, the buyer must do some investigations.[214]

When it comes to *non-negotiable claims (receivables)* there is only one possibility for a good faith acquisition. A good faith acquisition is possible after a double sale. The buyer must then in good faith give notice to the debtor before the first acquirer gives notice.[215]

Some *registered movables* are dealt with differently. The rules vary for different types of assets. There are special such rules for ships. Ships are registered movables.[216]

*Money* is not regulated by any special act. Money could be described as a negotiable instrument, but it would be more suitable to say that money is a special kind of asset since it is generic and the tool for exchange. The rightful owner can not claim the same money, only a certain amount, and this claim would in principle not be protected against other creditors, compare above (5.6.).

*Art* is considered to be tangibles and regulated through the ordinary rules.

---

[213] Promissory Notes Act 14 §.

[214] Promissory Notes Act 14 §.

[215] Promissory Notes Act 31 §.

[216] See Maritime Code (Sjölagen) chapter 2.

*Bulks* are also regulated as tangibles. To make a good faith acquisition it must be separated and delivered/transferred.

### 11.1.2. Seller's right was limited

It is possible to elaborate several different cases where the seller sale has infringed the right of someone else. The seller's right to dispose could for example be avoided retroactively, terminated by the first seller, sold twice etc. As said above there has however not generally been made any difference between different grounds for opposing the acquisition of C. It has not mattered what the ground has been for the inaccuracy of the seller. If the seller has possession of the good the buyer can make a good faith acquisition. A good faith acquisition could therefore occur in all the situations asked for.[217]

In case of termination of the contract A–B on account of non-payment (asset has been delivered to B) C does not have to be in good faith. If A made no retention of title, B is unhindered to sell and C does not have to be in good faith. It is however important that B is unauthorized to sell if there is a "retention of title" clause in the contract. In that case C must have been in good faith in order to acquire priority before A.

### 11.1.3. A terminological remark – "ownership" used functionally

A general terminological remark is that the Act of Good Faith Acquisitions from 1986 actually uses the word "ownership" and states that the acquirer gets "ownership" if he wins. In the Promissory Notes Act from 1936 the wording is instead that the acquirer should "be seen as the right creditor" and that the acquirer gets "priority". The difference in wording could be explained by the fact that the term "ownership" has often been avoided for objects that are claims. To use the term concerning tangibles is more unproblematic and in most respects a good description of the acquirer's position, although then a court decides upon these matters they will usually not express themselves as awarding the acquirer "ownership", but rather a "better right" to the good. It should be noted that it is not considered to be any difference in real whatever terminology you use. The remarks given here are however an example of an ambition to be careful with the use of the term "ownership" since it projects different kinds of consequential beliefs.

It could here also be reason to make a remark about the ownership terminology. As has been pointed out numerous times, the Scandinavian approach tries to avoid the term "ownership" as far as possible and seeks to develop separate suitable rules for all the aspects involved. When it comes to good faith acquisition it could

[217] Concerning double sales see section 6 above.

seem that what is acquired is – ownership (at one specific point in time and all aspects all together!) However, it must be kept in mind that such a description would be of no use with a Swedish approach. Descriptions, definitions and terminology are used to simplify communication, but to do that a description must communicate something that you earlier have acknowledged to be relevant. So even if it would have been a correct observation that an ownership is transferred at one specific point in time such a description is just simply useless.
Furthermore – if an ownership description would be made – it is true that the Act of Good Faith Acquisitions expressly states that it is the ownership that is acquired. But, when the requirements in the Act are fulfilled the good faith acquirer has also fulfilled the requirement for protection against the owner's creditors, i.e. the tradition requirement. In line with this the Act of Good Faith Acquisitions cannot be said to establish a unitary concept of ownership. It is rather the fact that the requirements for good faith acquisitions and protection against the seller's creditors often *converge* that might lead to the conclusion that a good faith acquisition according to the Act of Good Faith regulates all aspects of ownership. To illustrate the separation between good faith acquisitions and protection against the seller's creditors we could imagine that a notice filing system for protection against the creditors was introduced in Sweden, without any changes in the Act of Good Faith Acquisitions. Then there could be cases where the acquirer is protected from the rightful owner but not from his creditors. Moreover, after the changes in the Act of Good Faith 1 July 2003 it is not possible to make good faith acquisitions of stolen goods. The acquirer is protected from the seller's creditors when the tradition has taken place, but not against the rightful owner.

### 11.2. In effect only for value and price paid

The different rules for good faith acquisitions do generally treat sales, barter, gifts and transfer of security rights in the same way.[218]
Acquisitions through inheritance, bequest by last will and division of joint property between husband and wife are treated differently. These forms cannot be ground for a good faith acquisition.[219]
It must be noted that the right of redemption of tangibles is of decisive importance for gifts. Since the rightful owner can claim redemption for the lowest of the prize paid or the market value of the goods, a good faith acquisition through a gift would be of little value. The rightful owner can claim the goods in exchange for nothing as long as the acquirer has not had costs for the goods.[220]

---

[218] E.g. Håstad 1996, p 62ff.
[219] E.g. Håstad 1996, p 65.
[220] Act of Good Faith Acquisition.

If the tangible has not yet been paid for, the rightful owner can also claim the goods in exchange for nothing. At least that would be an effect of the said lowest value principle. In a case where the buyer has only paid partially the redemption prize would accordingly also be what has been paid.

### 11.3. Possession of the transferor

As said, possession or in other words physical control is needed. The "legitimizing appearance of possession" is the main argument used to motivate this principle.[221]

As said above the description different "forms of possession" is not very much used. The different acts for good faith acquisitions in general just use the term "possession". It could however be argued that possession through a third party should not be sufficient if the third party should know that the wrongful seller had no right to sell.[222]

### 11.4. Possession by the acquirer

As said possession, or in other words physical control, is needed also for the acquirer. For claims (receivables) "possession", or in other words priority, is reached through notice to the debtor. The motive is mainly to minimize the risks for multiple transactions from a person in need. It is argued that the acquirer will strive for possession if his priority is dependant of it and that this cutting off will deprive the transferor from the possibilities to transfer the goods further. This argumentation is combined with the view that the acquirer has no ground for feeling safe against a rightful owner if he and the rightful owner both have a claim to get the goods from the seller.[223]

It is argued that a third party should be able to hold the goods for the acquirer after the transfer even if the third party held the goods for the seller before.[224] A good question is if the third party has to be in good faith. The views vary.[225]

As said the description "forms of tradition" is seldom used. What has just been said about third party holders applies also for receivables where notice to the debtor is required.[226]

Since physical control is needed also for the acquirer constitutum possessorium is not an acknowledged possibility.[227]

---

[221] E.g. Håstad 1996, p 65.
[222] Compare Håstad 1996, p 66.
[223] E.g. Håstad 1996, p 66.
[224] E.g. Håstad 1996, p 66.
[225] Håstad 1996, p 66f. Helander, Bo: Kreditsäkerhet i lös egendom, 1984, p 458.
[226] Promissory Notes Act (Skuldebrevslagen) § 31.
[227] E.g. Håstad 1996, p 66.

### 11.5. Specific requirements regarding the "transferor"

As said, generally no difference is made between different kinds of transferors. It is not necessary that the original owner has "entrusted" the asset to the "transferor"? Nor it is necessary that the goods are sold in "ordinary business" or an auction. For tangibles a difference is however made between sellers who got possession through possession breaking crimes and others.[228]

### 11.6. Good faith

#### 11.6.1. Object of good faith

The wording of the rules concerning acquisition in good faith expresses that it is enough to believe that the transferor is entitled to dispose.[229] Accordingly there is no specific requirement for good faith concerning the transferor's right of ownership.

There are however also general rules for contracting through agents. These rules are applicable when the acquirer ought to have understood that the agent was not acting for himself. The principal are not bound if the agent exceeds the authority he is given by a written message. If, however, the agent exceeds internal, additional orders from the principal, the acquirer can nevertheless claim that the contract is binding, provided that he is in good faith. The fact that the agent goes beyond additional orders from the principal should not burden a counterpart in good faith.[230] However, if the agent's assignment is based on a verbal message from the principal, the acquirer can never make a good faith acquisition. An acquirer that relies on the agent's statement about his assignment only, will have to accept that all internal orders from the principal to the agent will be valid.

The line between the good faith acquisition rules and the rules for contracting by agents is in principle drawn by what the acquirer ought to have understood. If the agent says or acts as if he is the owner, the good faith acquisition rules apply. (It could however be discussed if it under any circumstances would be possible to use the rules for acquisition in good faith when the acquirer ought to have understood that the agent was not acting for himself.)[231]

[228] See above section 11.1.
[229] See section 6 and below 'standard of good faith'.
[230] Act of Contract § 10–11.
[231] SOU 1984:16.

### 11.6.2. Standard of good faith

Since the rule concerning tangibles in the Act of Good Faith Acquisitions, have been criticised and discussed to a large extent, the rule have been changed to sharpen the application of the rule by the courts, the police and the insurance companies. The wording is nowadays (since 1999): "An acquirer should be seen to have been in good faith only if it is probable, considering the kind of tangible, the circumstances under which the sale took place, and the circumstances in general, that the acquirer should not have suspected that the transferor was not entitled to dispose." From precedence it is quite clear that there is a strong burden of investigation on the acquirer for some kinds of property as cars. Especially if it the acquirer is a professional dealer.[232]

The rules for negotiable instruments and receivables are not as sharp. The rule for receivables just states that "good faith" is necessary.[233] The different rules for negotiable instruments vary from what could be described as gross negligence to negligence.[234]

### 11.6.3. Time when good faith is required

As said (see 11.1.) the acquirer must still be in good faith at the time of delivery, respectively the time of notice.

### 11.6.4. Burden of proof – no presumption of good faith

A useful description would be that there is a presumption in favour of the rightful owner. It is the acquirer who has the burden of proof and has to show, depending on the kind of asset, that he should not have suspected anything, that he was in good faith or that he was not negligent.[235]

### 11.6.5. Duty to inform

There are no formal rules for any additional requirements. The additional requirements all stem from the general balance of interests and the circumstances in the specific situation. A description like a "duty to inform" the original owner about the circumstances of the acquisition would not be relevant. As said there are however precedence that makes it quite clear that there is a strong burden of investigation on the acquirer for some kinds of property. If there is a practical possibility to make investigations the acquirer should do so. In this way it is an

---

[232] E.g. Håstad 1996, p 67ff.

[233] Promissory Notes Act (Skuldebrevslagen) § 31.

[234] Promissory Notes Act (Skuldebrevslagen) § 14.

[235] E.g. Håstad 1996, p 68.

ordinary additional requirement to check a register if there is a register available, as for cars and boats.[236]

## 11.7. Lost goods, stolen goods etc

As said (see 11.1.) a difference is nowadays made between sellers who got possession to a tangible through possession breaking crimes as theft or robbery and sellers who got possession through other ways as lease, lending, deceit, usury etc. The wording of the definition is: "taken unauthorised, by force on a person or by threat of violence which for the victim appears as a direct danger".[237]
The motive to give stronger protection to the rightful owner concerning goods lost by possession breaking crime, is as said (see 11.1.), that it has been regarded as unfair and unjust to let the acquirer win. Even though there has been a rather wide right of redemption, the former solution was by many seen as something immoral. It was also argued that the former solution facilitated some kinds of criminal activity.[238]

## 11.8. Right of the original owner to buy back the asset

As said (see 11.1.) the right of redemption can be used in all cases concerning tangibles. It is even possible to use after a double sale.
The right of redemption applies to anybody. (One concern behind the law was to protect museums and other public bodies of common interest. A museum should be able to get the goods back if it shows up after fifty years. No private body should be protected against such a common interest.)[239]
The original (or rightful) owner has the right to pay the good faith acquirer the lowest amount of what the good faith acquirer paid plus whatever he has paid to improve the goods, or the market price. Inflation should be considered when calculating the redemption sum.[240]
When the original owner pays the redemption sum he has the right to get the property delivered in exchange. The question when the original owner re-acquires his property is not relevant with a functional approach.
If C becomes insolvent A would probably have priority against C's creditors. Since the property is specified A should be able to separate it if he pays the redemption sum.

---

236 E.g. Håstad 1996, p 67ff. NJA 1989 s 784, NJA 1993 s 429, NJA 1995 s 337.
237 Act of Good Faith Acquisition § 3.
238 Proposition 2002/03:17 p 15.
239 SOU 1984:16.
240 Act of Good Faith Acquisition § 6.

As said (see 11.1.) there is a six months limit for redemption. These six months begin at the moment when the rightful owner ought to have known that the goods were in the possession of the acquirer.[241]
There are as said also a 10-year limit for the possibility to claim goods that the rightful owner have been deprived of through possession breaking crimes. After that period he has only a right of redemption in exchange for the redemption sum.[242]

11.9. Other property rights than ownership

If a person buys a movable from the owner or a person who possesses the authority to dispose of the movable, but the movable is encumbered with a security right of a third party the same rules generally apply. As said (see 11.1.) security rights are treated as ownership rights are treated.
Usufructary rights are treated differently and it could be argued that they should in principle not be protected. It could however also be argued that they should be protected. The normative arguments for not protecting them are old (see 2.1.2.). It is also practically possible to create protection by using a security right in combination with the usufructuary right. The lessee is then given the right to use the goods as a security to get paid for any damages that a contract-breaching sale will generate.[243]

## 12. "Acquisitative" prescription

As said (see 2.1.) rights in rem are with a few exceptions not subject to limitation. The description limitation, acquisitive prescription, or "Ersitzung" is seldom used for movables. The Swedish term for "Ersitzung" (hävd) is only used concerning real estate. However, the description is useful to describe a few phenomena also for movables and from the 1 July 2003 it is used in the Act of Good Faith Acquisitions.
There is now (see 11.1. and 11.8.) a limitation of ten years for the right to claim goods that the rightful owner has been deprived of through possession breaking crimes. There is however still a right of redemption even after these ten years.[244]
Another case of limitation concerns retention of title. The right in rem is limited in exactly the same way as the claim for the price. When the seller's claim is

[241] Act of Good Faith Acquisition § 5.
[242] Act of Good Faith Acquisition § 4–5.
[243] Håstad 1996, p 237-238.
[244] Act of Good Faith Acquisition §§ 4-5.

prescribed he cannot claim the sold good either.[245] The general limitation period is ten years. For non-negotiable claims against consumers the limit is three years.[246]

## 13. Reservation of title

As said (see 6.13.) reservation, or retention, of title is done through a contractual condition. It is generally agreed that such a condition must be made before delivery. There is no formality required to have the condition in writing, but a document does of course facilitate when it comes to the point where evidence must be given.[247] Registration is neither necessary nor possible, but is sometimes used for informative reasons, such as in the car register.

With a Swedish or Scandinavian approach it is the right to *take the goods back* that is retained. The Swedish term for retention of title is "retaking right", but the terminology is not important – the aims of the parties and the function are decisive. It is nowadays considered silly to make a difference between a contractual term that states retention of title / "ownership" and a term that says that the seller should have the possibility to take the good back if the buyer does not pay.[248]

If a categorisation would be of any use the choice would probably be to define retention of title as a security right. (The Norwegian Act of Securities uses the term "sale security" – salgspant).

What is important is however not the categorisation but the effects that retention of title brings. If the seller takes the goods back he must give the buyer back what he has paid, minus expenses. That is also the case in a bankruptcy for the buyer, but a practical solution is then sometimes that the administrator buys the property for the estate.

As said (see 6.8.) the buyer is also under a penal obligation not to sell, pawn or otherwise dispose of the good. As long as the goods are not paid for, the buyer's creditors must also first pay the seller before they can demand the enforcement service to sell the good for their credits. The seller gets priority over the creditors.

As also said (see 10.) it could be stressed that the solutions concerning speciality probably differs between retention of title cases and other cases as stolen, lent and rented property. Sellers are not given priority except in situations where it is easy

---

245 Credit Sales of Goods Act (Avbetalningsköplagen) § 7.

246 Act of Limitation (Preskriptionslagen) § 2.

247 E.g. Håstad 1996, p 180ff. For consumers the retention of title must nowadays be in writing according to a general rule concerning conditions for consumer credits, see Consumer Credit Act § 9.

248 Hessler, Henrik: Om äganderättsförbehåll och återtagandeförbehåll i 1966 års lag om vad som är fast egendom, in Nordisk Gjenklang Festskrift till Arnholm, 1969, p 459–473, especially p 470–473 where he dismisses the view that the word ownership or such must be used, as a call for magic.

and cost effective to take the good back. Compared to some other European systems the Swedish retention of title institute is rather limited (see 6.8.). In cases of *accessio, confusion, commixtio* and *specificatio* the seller will loose his right and have a claim for money only.

If the buyer sells the property without the seller's permission it would be possible to argue that the seller's right also should cover the proceeds of a resale. There is no rule that states such a solution and the seller can in principle not turn to the buyer's buyer (C). The seller can however turn to the first buyer and claim priority by the general surrogation principle (surrogationsprincipen).[249] If the buyer sells the goods (just) before a bankruptcy, the seller could argue that he should have priority concerning a sum of money that can be identified as a surrogate for the goods and that still is amongst the belongings of the buyer. The seller could in other words claim priority to the proceeds.

[249] Håstad 1996, p 164ff. Walin, Gösta: Separationsrätt, p 162ff.

## Part IV: Co-ownership

### 14. Co-ownership

As said (see 10.) co-ownership can be used as a solution to the problems where the acquirer combines or mixes the goods in a way that the transferor's right in rem is lost. The question is discussed, but a clear doctrine has not been elaborated.[250]

The general rules concerning co-ownership are set out in the 1904 Act of Co-ownership. This act deals with the internal problems between co-owners and the solutions are 1) that a co-owner can demand that an administrator should manage the property until the co-owners can agree, and 2) that the property should be sold by the administrator if the co-owners don not agree.

There are no special rules concerning transfer of a co-ownership share.[251] The ordinary rules concerning the binding of parties, risk and responsibility will guide the solutions.

As mentioned (see 6.9.) the courts have in some cases created notice requirements for priority against the creditors. It has been discussed if it should be enough to give notice to one of these parties or to all of them. If it is clear to everybody which one of these third parties who should be given notice, it can be argued that it is an effective solution that notice is given only to this party.[252]

---

[250] Compare Håstad 1996, p 174.
[251] Håstad 1996, p 55.
[252] Martinson 2002, p 313–315.

## Salzburger Studien zum Europäischen Privatrecht

Herausgegeben von J. Michael Rainer

Band 1 Marc Herzog: Die Haftung des Gastwirts für eingebrachte Sachen des Gasts nach §§ 701 - 703 des Deutschen Bürgerlichen Gesetzbuchs. 1999.

Band 2 Andreas Reinhart: Familienplanungsschaden. Wrongful birth, wrongful life, wrongful conception, wrongful pregnancy. Eine rechtsvergleichende Untersuchung anhand des deutschen und des anglo-amerikanischen Rechts. 1999.

Band 3 Markus Frank: Untersuchungen zu den *Politika* des Aristoteles. 1999.

Band 4 Stefan Josef Schermaier: Der Gemeinschaftsrechtliche Staatshaftungsanspruch. Entwicklung, Perspektiven und Auswirkungen auf das österreichische Recht. 1999.

Band 5 Carmen Windhaber: Reiserecht in Österreich, Deutschland und Kanada. 2000.

Band 6 Korbinian Dietl: Unfallhaftung beim Expeditions- und Trekkingbergsteigen. Zugleich ein Beitrag zum Reiserecht für den Bereich der Bergreisen sowie zum Sporthaftungsrecht für den Bereich des Bergsports. 2000.

Band 7 Erich Jeroscheg: Eigentum an beweglichen Sachen. Französisches Recht und Rechtsvergleich. 2000.

Band 8 Thomas Tschaler: Das Moment der Gefahr als Element der Schadenszurechnung im System des Haftpflichtrechts. Eine rechtstheoretische Untersuchung der möglichen Schwächen gängiger Haftungsmodelle. 2000.

Band 9 Christian Hellenthal: Zulässigkeit einer supranationalen Fußball-Europaliga nach den Bestimmungen des europäischen Wettbewerbsrechts. 2000.

Band 10 Wolfgang Bengen: Die Systematik des § 823 I BGB im Deliktsrecht. Zugleich ein Beitrag zu den Verkehrspflichten. 2000.

Band 11 Gerhard Pöttler: Vergleichende Verbraucherschutzrichtlinienumsetzung in europäischen Mitgliedsstaaten. Anhand ausgewählter Beispiele der Pauschalreise-, Timesharing- und Produkthaftungsrichtlinie. 2001.

Band 12 Johannes Michael Rainer: Europäisches Privatrecht. Die Rechtsvergleichung. 2002.

Band 13 Erwin Schön: Allgemeines Vertragsrecht und Kaufvertragsrecht - ein Rechtsvergleich Österreich, USA, Spanien und UN-Kaufrecht. Unter Einbeziehung von PECL und UNIDROIT-Prinzipien. Gemeinsamkeiten, Unterschiede, Bewertungsversuche. 2003.

Band 14 Patrick Schenner: Skiunfall! Wer haftet? Schadenersatz im österreichischen Skirecht. 2003.

Band 15 Peter Unterkofler: Die rechtliche Stellung des Pflichtteilsberechtigten im Spannungsverhältnis zwischen Erbrecht und Privatstiftungsrecht. 2003.

Band 16 Susanne Spaun: Der Herausgabeanspruch bei Diebstahl oder illegalem Export von Kulturgütern. 2003.

Band 17 Josef Wolff: Trust, Fiducia und fiduziarische Treuhand. Historisch-rechtsvergleichende Untersuchung mit einer Darstellung des Trust in Schottland sowie des römischen und österreichischen Fideikommiss. 2005.

Band 18 Johannes Michael Rainer / Johanna Filip-Fröschl: Transfer of Title Concerning Movables Part I – Eigentumsübertragung an beweglichen Sachen in Europa Teil I. Introduction, Estonia, Italy, Poland, Portugal, Scotland, Slovenia. Einführung, Estland, Italien, Polen, Portugal, Schottland, Slowenien. Edited by Johannes Michael Rainer – Herausgegeben von Johannes Michael Rainer. 2006.

Band 19 Mary-Rose McGuire: Transfer of Title Concerning Movables Part II – Eigentumsübertragung an beweglichen Sachen in Europa Teil II. National Report: Germany. Edited by Johannes Michael Rainer – Herausgegeben von Johannes Michael Rainer. 2006.

Band 20 Claes Martinson: Transfer of Title Concerning Movables Part III – Eigentumsübertragung an beweglichen Sachen in Europa Teil III. National Report: Sweden. Edited by Johannes Michael Rainer – Herausgegeben von Johannes Michael Rainer. 2006.

Band 21 Arthur Salomons: Transfer of Title Concerning Movables Part IV – Eigentumsübertragung an beweglichen Sachen in Europa Teil IV. National Report: The Netherlands. Edited by Johannes Michael Rainer – Herausgegeben von Johannes Michael Rainer. 2006.

www.peterlang.de